Airport Landscape

Sonja Dümpelmann, Charles Waldheim (eds.)

Urban Ecologies in the Aerial Age

Airport Landscape

Sonja Dümpelmann, Charles Waldheim (eds.)

Urban Ecologies in the Aerial Age

Foreword

Robert De Niro and Al Pacino on the airfield of LAX during the final scene of *Heat*, 1995.

Most of us are familiar with the almost invariable routine of landing at a major airport: deplane, walk along a wide corridor past many arrival and departure gates, go down an escalator, catch a shuttle train, proceed through immigration, collect baggage, pass under a set of escalators, catch another train, and exit the airport. It is only when you have truly left the airport building behind you—when the train has gone through a series of tunnels and emerged into daylight or the glare of nighttime lights—that you might begin to have some sense of the landscape that surrounds you, of greenery, industrial buildings, streets, houses, and back gardens.

For many of us, the experience of the airport is one of being cocooned, of being contained within a massive mechanized interconnected interior and not seeing anything of the outside. The airport and its alienating characteristics have been the subject of many reflections, none of them more widely discussed than *Non-Places: An Introduction to Supermodernity* by the French anthropologist Marc Augé. But not everyone responds to travel and airports the same way. As portrayed in the 2009 film *Up in the Air*, airports are perhaps not as much of a non-place as Augé would have us believe. Through the eyes of a perpetually traveling corporate downsizer (played by George Clooney), we see a different world—one with a specific organizational structure built on frequent-flyer miles, seating upgrades, and membership-only lounges that construct their own codes of conduct, desires, hierarchies, and meaning.

Another contradiction to the idea that the airport is a non-place is the experience that occurs while you are still on a plane and approaching your destination. As the plane descends, you see the landscape surrounding the airport come closer and closer. The rapidly moving close-up of the terrain is an uncommon optical experience of changing scale—a kind of reversal of the 1977 film by Charles and Ray Eames, *Powers of Ten*, which zooms out from a picnic scene on the ground to depict larger and larger parts of the earth in quick succession.

The fact that the airplane often provides one of the best views of the airport landscape represents a major shift from the early days of commercial aviation, when the

Robert De Niro and Al Pacino on the airfield of LAX during the final scene of *Heat*, 1995.

visible relationship between the passenger terminal and the runway was an important part of the experience of the airport, even for those not traveling. I remember people going to the airport—voluntarily—just to visit the restaurant and enjoy the vast animated vista of runways, with the carefully choreographed mechanical performance of planes landing and taking off for exotic locations.

Ironically, flying at night can be one of the most exhilarating ways to experience airports and their surrounding landscapes. If your destination is a big city, the approach can bring a dazzling display of landmarks, buildings, and streets. Often the aerial view of a city at night shows its activities and movements in sharper relief. But perhaps the most mesmerizing—and surreal—view of all is that of the airport and its runways at night. What might appear like a natural landscape during the day is transformed, through illumination, into pure artifice. This use of night lighting to construct a specific form of artificial terrain is something that landscape architecture has not yet managed to utilize opportunistically during the development of its ideas. Such a construction depends on a more distinct articulation of the differences between the landscapes of night and day.

One of the best demonstrations of these landscapes of light can be found in the closing minutes of Michael Mann's 1995 movie *Heat*, which move from a hotel on the edge of Los Angeles airport, LAX, onto the airfield, where the character played by Robert De Niro is being chased by Al Pacino, as a police officer. During these scenes the airport landscape is the backdrop for the action, but the action—the characters and their movements—is also a catalyst for showing the airport landscape, both close and far. Rather than relying solely on the general lighting of the airport, which can be quite dark on the periphery, Mann uses the lights of the airplanes on the runway to construct fleeting moments of stillness and suspense when the landscape changes in an instant from dark to light, revealing aspects of both the action and the setting.

The scenes from the movie are evocations of an airport landscape. They produce temporal moments of material and performative juxtaposition; close-up shots of a container behind which De Niro's character hides are cut against the bulk of the plane and the vast landscape of the airport. While these images produce a new representation of LAX, they also offer clues about ways in which one might construct new airport landscapes. Such procedures are particularly relevant now that so many decommissioned and abandoned airports are going through a process of revitalization. How can these airports become new productive public spaces, and how can landscape be the agent of change in that process? This book seeks to answer these questions and others.

Mohsen Mostafavi

Preface

This book presents the airport as a site of and for landscape, featuring a collection of seminal design projects and innovative landscape management strategies for operating and decommissioned airports. In assembling this material, we assume an augmented role for landscape architects commensurate with their status as urbanists of the aerial age.

In addition to our two essays, canonical work has been selected to support this claim. The book is organized within two main thematic categories: Operations and Afterlives. Projects included in Airport Operations epitomize the standing of landscape as a design medium for operating airports. In addition, particular animal and plant species that play an important role in the landscape management of various airports are featured. They are complemented by the presentation of certain objects that characterize the airport landscape, such as windsocks and sound cannons. The projects grouped in Airport Afterlives speak to the agency of landscape as a medium of design for imagining the future of abandoned airports. These projects are arranged according to five themes that have also been central to the disciplinary formation of landscape architecture: Production, Urbanity, Succession, Topography, and Restoration.

In the last quarter-century, the airport has not only regained significant attention from landscape architects; it has also attracted a number of photographers, 10 of whom are featured here. Their work offers additional insight into how we see and inhabit the airport landscape. Together, the material gathered in this volume attests to the airport's enduring significance as a site for contemporary urban culture.

Sonja Dümpelmann
Charles Waldheim

Acknowledgments

This book draws from material developed for the exhibition "Airport Landscape: Urban Ecologies in the Aerial Age" held at the Harvard University Graduate School of Design in the fall of 2013. We would like to thank Dean Mohsen Mostafavi for his support of both the exhibition and the publication. The Graham Foundation for Advanced Studies in the Fine Arts provided crucial support for the exhibition, and the GSD's John E. (Jack) Irving Dean's Innovation Fund and Scruggs Fund contributed to the realization of this book.

We thank graphic designer Siena Scarff for her work on the exhibition and a digital precursor to this volume, and Sam de Groot for his graphic design of this book. We also are indebted to the Department of Exhibitions led by Dan Borelli and to our colleagues in the Frances Loeb Library—Irina Gorstein, Johanna Kasubowski, Ardys Kozbial, Alix Reiskind, and Inés Zalduendo—for their help in realizing the exhibition.

At the GSD, we also thank Pat Roberts, Beth Kramer, Ann Whiteside, Benjamin Prosky, Sara Gothard, Anne Mathew, and Nicole Sander. Further thanks go to our faculty colleagues Silvia Benedito, Anita Berrizbeitia, Luis Callejas, Kelly Doran, Robert Pietrusko, Chris Reed, and Allen Sayegh.

We would like to thank the following students for their support: Dalal Musaed Alsayer, Azzurra Cox, Emily Drury, Kelly Fleming, Ateya Khorakiwala, Lisl Kotheimer, Fadi Masoud, and Ostap Rudakevych.

We greatly appreciate the engaged collaboration of the designers and photographers who provided information and insights into the projects profiled here. We are equally grateful to a number of firms and individuals who generously supplied information and material, but whose work we were unable to feature given limitations of space. Big thanks also go to Jennifer Sigler and Melissa Vaughn. Without their generous commitment of time and energy, this project would not have been possible.

Claiming the Airport as Landscape

Charles Waldheim

If the erasure of conventional boundaries is the most salient spatial feature of the late-twentieth-century condition, the airport may be taken as its most perfect landscape expression.
—Denis Cosgrove, 1990[1]

Airports have never been more central to the life of cities, yet they remain largely peripheral in design culture. In spite of this marginal status, landscape architects have recently reasserted their historic claims on the airfield as a site of design through a range of practices. This publication presents these practices and convenes a discussion of the airport as landscape that draws on a variety of disciplinary perspectives.

Over the past decade, the airport has emerged as a central venue and case study in the discourse surrounding landscape urbanism. It is equally fundamental to the aspirations of emergent discourse under the rubric of ecological urbanism. The deployment of landscape as an operating system for contemporary urbanism is manifested through an impressive array of projects for both operating and abandoned airports over the past two decades. In addition to highly visible and influential competitions such as Downsview Park Toronto and Hellinikon International Airport in Athens, a number of studies have been made for smaller sites such as Floyd Bennett Field in New York and Northerly Island in Chicago. A strong body of built precedent has

1   Denis Cosgrove (with paintings by Adrian Hemming), "Airport/Landscape," in *Recovering Landscape: Essays in Contemporary Landscape Architecture*, ed. James Corner (New York: Princeton Architectural Press, 1999), 227. In referring to "the erasure of conventional boundaries as the most salient spatial feature of the late-twentieth-century condition," Cosgrove cites David Harvey's seminal argument on the role of capital in cultural change. Harvey, *The Condition of Postmodernity: An Enquiry into the Origins of Cultural Change* (Cambridge, MA: Blackwell, 1989).

emerged in Western Europe and Scandinavia, with several significant examples in Germany and Norway. Competitions for airport sites as varied as Vatnsmýri, Iceland; Casablanca, Morocco; Quito, Ecuador; and Taichung, Taiwan, have underscored the relevance of the topic for international audiences.

Airports occupy pivotal positions in the geographies, economies, and ecologies of the cities they continue to shape. In spite of this centrality, the airport inhabits a cultural blind spot, one characterized by a categorical confusion over how best to think about the airport. In many contexts, the airport is relegated to a kind of cultural denial. Into this void, landscape architecture has recently reasserted its historic claims to the airfield as a landscape. As my colleague and co-editor Sonja Dümpelmann's recent publication *Flights of Imagination* asserts, this embrace by landscape architecture of the airport is a return to the historic origins of the airfield as a landscape condition.[2]

Although it may initially appear counterintuitive to read an airport as landscape, further consideration reveals the impossibility of adequately conceiving the contemporary airport site as either a building or simply urban infrastructure. It may be productive to regard the airport as a work of architecture, or an urban assemblage, yet its relentless horizontality and evacuation of human occupation resist this interpretation. Many attempts to cloak the airport in architectural or urban guise reveal a troubling tendency, as if the language of the 19th century could camouflage the airport, making it more acceptable as an urban form.

Yet this desire for an architectonic or urban alibi runs counter to the structural spatial conditions of the airport. What is a modern jet-age airport if not a contiguous, highly choreographed, scrupulously maintained, and continuously monitored landscape? In this sense, Cosgrove's characterization of the airport as landscape has less to do with the material of landscape than with its capacity to present a synoptic and coherent spatial synthesis of otherwise disparate technical, cultural, and biological dimensions. As he described London's Heathrow: "a space that may initially seem to lie well beyond the conventional understanding of what constitutes a landscape...We are not here concerned with such design issues as landscaping the terminals, runways, or public open spaces but rather with conceiving the airport as a complex functional, spatial, and, to a degree, visual whole."[3]

This reading of the airport as landscape can be found across a broad range of cultural forms, from painting through film, though it is perhaps most indelibly captured via photography. French aerial photographer Yann Arthus-Bertrand has assembled a compelling range of images of the operating surfaces of runways and taxiways taken from a helicopter hovering above the airfield. American photographer Phil Underdown has produced haunting images of abandoned airfields overtaken by spontaneous vegetation and returning to a post-urban wild.[4] These photographs, and other visual representations of the airport in painting or film, reveal the airport landscape juxtaposing the technical space of aviation with traces of human agency and biological function. These images often invoke relations between human and non-human, real and fake. As such, cultural images of the operating or abandoned airfield can often, paradoxically, present the airport as a landscape more effectively than the

2 On the subject of the origins of the airfield as landscape and the impact of aviation on landscape architecture, see Sonja Dümpelmann's excellent history of the subject, *Flights of Imagination: Aviation, Landscape, Design* (Charlottesville, VA: University of Virginia Press, 2014).

3 Cosgrove, "Airport/Landscape," 221–222.

4 See photographic portfolios by Yann Arthus-Bertrand, Phil Underdown, and others in this publication.

direct, unmediated experience of the same site. These representations are also capable of presenting the uncanny quality of the airport's enormous evacuated horizontality.

The overwhelming majority of the modern airport is given over to "airside" operations—a vast horizontal surface set aside as margin of error for contingencies including future expansions; environmental management of adjacent environments; protection for and from surrounding communities and their residents; and aircraft operations themselves. The creation of this tremendous vacuity removes not only human occupation but scrubs the airfield of virtually all remnants of previous hydrological and biological processes. Managing the resultant denuded surfaces becomes a central concern for airport operations and contributes further to the sense of estrangement and alienation that the airfield engenders.

Airports tend to be planned for sites far from the cities that they serve, yet they often become the center of the metropolitan areas they in part create. This fact renders the airport's engineered emptiness central to questions of urban life and spatial experience; the airport is an increasingly significant surrogate for the contemporary centerless city itself. These two fundamental and organic conditions of the modern airport—its internal set-aside of space and its relative remoteness from the city that it enables—conspire to produce a "non-site." French anthropologist Marc Augé has described this condition and the modern airport as a "non-lieux" or "non-place" associated with advanced modernization or what he describes as "supermodernity."[5] Three decades prior to Augé's formulation of the airport as a "non-lieux," the Dutch artist and

theorist Constant Nieuwenhuys placed the airport in a specific temporal relation to the shape of the city. Constant described the modern airport as an anticipation of the "city of the future," and an itinerant urbanism of "man simply passing through."[6]

Another architect to explicitly read the modern airport as a vast public landscape was Alvin Boyarsky, chair of the Architectural Association School of Architecture. Boyarsky had previously taught at the University of Illinois in Chicago, where he encountered O'Hare International Airport as a vast public-works landscape. Boyarsky's formulation from over a half-century ago resonates with contemporary interests in landscape infrastructure and anticipates recent readings of the airport as landscape: "An inspiring diagram, speaking the poetry of flow, an unheralded masterpiece descended from such giant prototypical installations as the stockyards, the pier, the service tunnels, Soldiers Field, etc., it recalls the generic style of the city itself."[7]

The work of Robert Smithson offers another case study in the modern airport conceived as landscape. In 1966, Smithson was retained by Tippetts, Abbett, McCarthy & Stratton Engineers and Architects to serve as an "artist-consultant" for the design of the new Dallas/Fort Worth International Airport; he advised on the design of an aerial gallery/landscape that was intended to be experienced from the air as well as from the ground. The introduction of a gallery or museum as part of the terminal complex was meant to serve as a kind of curatorial or representational lens through which the aerial experience of the landscape could be read. Two articles by Smithson, "Towards the Development of an Air Terminal Site" and "Aerial Art," explored the

5 Marc Augé, *Non-Places: Introduction to an Anthropology of Supermodernity*, trans. John Howe (London: Verso, 1995).

6 Constant's full formulation was: "The airport of today can be seen as the anticipatory image of the city of tomorrow, the city of man 'passing through.'" Constant Nieuwenhuys, "On Traveling," trans. of "Over het reizen," 1966 (first published in Dutch in *Opstand van de Homo Ludens*, 1969). See also Mark Wigley, *Constant's New*

Babylon: The Hyper-Architecture of Desire* (Rotterdam: Witte de With, Center for Contemporary Art/010 publishers, 1998), 200–201.

7 Alvin Boyarsky, "Chicago à la Carte: The City as Energy System," *Architectural Design* 40 (December 1970): 595–640. In his original draft, Boyarsky made explicit reference to class at O'Hare, "O'Hare, Versailles to Chicago, where only the rich can circulate." This reference was elided in the more widely available

posthumous reprint of the essay in 1996. See Boyarsky, "Typescript Notes and Preliminary Draft of 'Chicago à la Carte: The City as Energy System,'" Boyarsky personal papers, courtesy Nicholas Boyarsky (1970): n.p.; and Boyarsky, "Chicago à la Carte: The City as Energy System," reprinted in *Architectural Associations: The Idea of the City*, ed. Robin Middleton (Cambridge, MA, London: MIT Press, Architectural Association, 1996), 10–49.

theoretical potential of these new forms of cultural production and reception. Smithson's interest in the dialectical relationship between the representation of a site within the gallery and the subsequent aerial experience of that site culminated in his development of the "non-site" as a representational and projective practice. Smithson's conception of aerial art and his formulation of the non-site as a representational mechanism warrant further investigation, as they postulate an aerial viewing subject for contemporary landscape practice.[8]

In the wake of Smithson's unrealized proposal for "aerial art," landscape architect Daniel Kiley was retained to execute a landscape plan for the site. Kiley produced a range of landscape projects specifically implicating an aerial subject. Among these, Kiley's landscape projects for Dallas/Fort Worth International Airport (1969) and Dulles International Airport (1955–58) are especially significant in the evolution of the Jet Age airport typology. Kiley also developed at least two aerial gardens designed to be experienced from the air as well as on the ground. These gardens deployed large pools connected by pathways and structured allées of trees. The first project, Kiley's Air Force Academy campus landscape plan (1954–62), in collaboration with Walter Netsch and Skidmore, Owings & Merrill, features a large central aerial garden as the centerpiece of the cadet campus.[9]

Based on his experience working with Kiley on the Air Force Academy project, Chicago architect Stan Gladych recommended Kiley to C. F. Murphy for the Jardine Water Filtration Plant project, an obscure public park and waterworks infrastructure on Chicago's lakefront. A previous scheme by Hideo Sasaki had been rejected as unfeasible. In this instance, the garden was to provide an aerial view for the "cliff-dwelling" residents of the Gold Coast's high-rise apartment buildings. The project included the landscape for the Jardine Plant itself as well as an adjacent public park. The park features a classical Kiley allée of locust trees extending toward the horizon and culminating in a cantilevered plane. The main structuring device of the park is a set of five large fountains, recalling the Great Lakes. These vast pools invoke the rhetorical dimension of the largely prosaic function of the water treatment facility. Kiley's design unites the public works facility with the public park through the representation of water as seen by an aerial viewing subject.[10]

The subject of the airport as a landscape has been reanimated in recent years within the discourse of landscape urbanism. The past decade has seen a number of high-profile projects for converting redundant airfields into public parks, often selected through international design competitions. The shift of the international airport serving Athens from the coastal airport site at Hellinikon to Mesogeia in 2001 opened a 530-hectare site to the Athenian public for use as a public park. An international competition invited proposals for the design of the park over its disused runways as well as the organization of future urban development around the edges of the site. This ambitious program proposed housing, commercial buildings, and cultural venues in the context of a vast horizontal stretch of land overlooking the sea.

The winning scheme, by Philippe Coignet/ Office of Landscape Morphology with DZO Architecture, Elena Fernandez, David Serero, Arnaud Descombes, and Antoine Regnault,

8   Robert Smithson, "Towards the Development of an Air Terminal Site," *Artforum*, no. 6 (June 1967): 36–40; and "Aerial Art," *Studio International*, no. 177 (April 1969): 180–181. This understanding of Smithson's interest in aerial representation has been illuminated by the research of Mark Linder. See Linder, "Sitely Windows: Robert Smithson's Architectural Criticism," *Assemblage*, no. 39 (1999): 6–35; which clarifies the relationship between Smithson's work as an "artist-consultant" to the Dallas/ Fort Worth International Airport and his subsequent development of the "non-site."

9   Dan Kiley and Jane Amidon, *Dan Kiley: The Complete Works of America's Master Landscape Architect* (Boston: Bulfinch Press, 1999); also see Dümpelmann, *Flights of Imagination*.

10   Kiley and Amidon, *Dan Kiley.*

James Corner Field Operations and Stan Allen,
Downsview Park Competition, Toronto, phasing and
emergence diagrams, 2000.

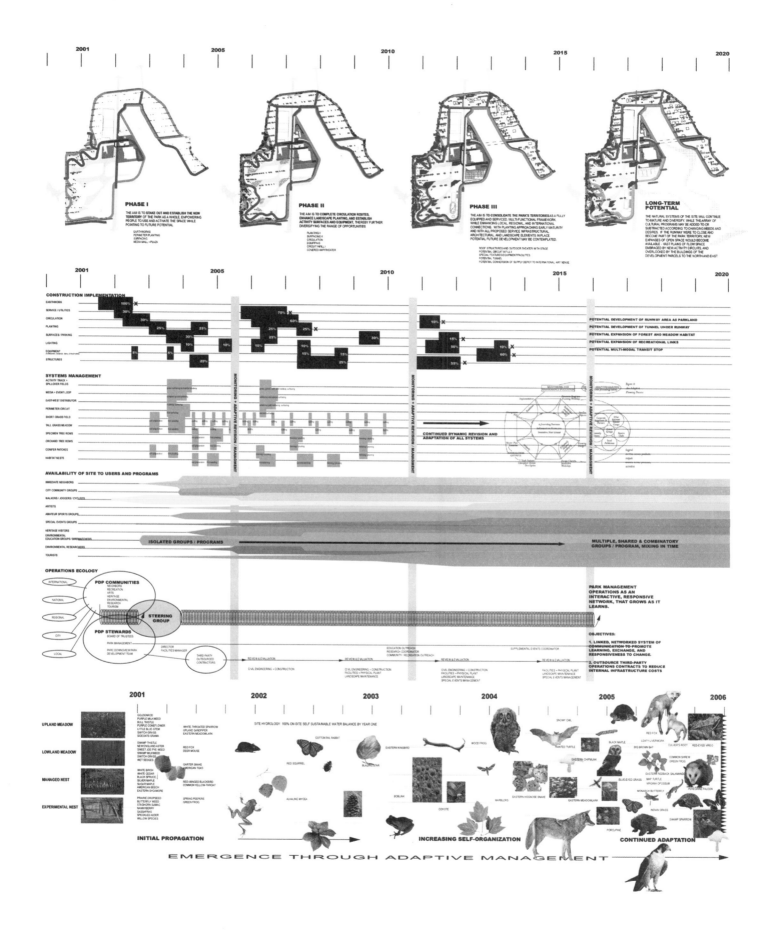

featured complex waveform landscape berms traversing the formerly flat airfield and reconnecting the higher-elevation neighborhoods with the coast below. This strategy of cut and fill, while reconciling the enormously scaled airfield with the spatial requirements of a distinctly designed landscape, also assists in delivering flows of fast-moving surface water and slow-moving visitors across the park. Throughout this topographic construction, a complex counterdiagram of succession planting is set in motion to register the shift of the park from an initially ordered arrangement that slowly gives way to a self-regulating arboreal ecosystem. Although the ambitious scheme remains unrealized, it offers a compelling case study in the potentials of landscape urbanism and the abandoned airport as public park.[11]

Downsview Park in Toronto was among the most ambitious of these initiatives for reclaiming abandoned airport sites, with a two-stage international design competition for a public park to be built on a former military airbase in the rapidly aging and no-longer-peripheral suburbs of Canada's most populous city. The Downsview project represented a portion of Canada's peace dividend from the end of the Cold War. The airbase was engaged for a variety of military aviation purposes during its half-century of use between the 1940s and its decommissioning in the 1990s, when its future came up for public discussion. Although the site was marginal to Toronto's pre–World War II population, postwar suburbanization engulfed the periphery, and Downsview now sits near the heart of the metropolitan area.

Almost inevitably, airfields tend to be sited on topographically and ecologically undistinguished terrain. Downsview is no exception. The airfield was designed to occupy the higher and drier, yet still relatively flat, open ground between two of the region's important watersheds: the Don River to the east and the Humber River to the west. The finalist project for Downsview by James Corner and Stan Allen exemplifies the potentials of the airport site as landscape park and is viewed as a canonical example of landscape urbanism. Emblematic of this project—and by now standard fare for projects of this type—are detailed diagrams of phasing, animal habitats, succession planting, and hydrological systems, as well as programmatic and planning regimes. Particularly compelling is the complex interweaving of natural ecologies with the social, cultural, and infrastructural layers of the contemporary city.[12]

Rem Koolhaas/OMA (with Bruce Mau) and Bernard Tschumi also submitted entries as finalists in the Downsview Park competition. In this project, they found their historical fortunes reversed from their roles as first- and second-place authors of the Parc de la Villette competition of two decades prior. The imageable and media-friendly Koolhaas/OMA and Mau scheme for Downsview, "Tree City," was awarded first prize and the commission; while the more sublime, layered, and intellectually challenging scheme of the office of Bernard Tschumi will doubtless enjoy greater ongoing influence within architectural culture, particularly as the information age transforms our understandings and limits of the "natural." Tschumi's "The Digital and the Coyote" presented an electronic analog to his longstanding interest in urban event, with richly detailed diagrams of succession planting and the seeding of ambient urbanity in the midst

11   See http://www.o-l-m.net/zoom-projet.php?id=40.

12   Julia Czerniak, ed., CASE: *Downsview Park Toronto* (Cambridge, MA, Munich: Harvard University Graduate School of Design, Prestel, 2001).

of seemingly desolate prairies. Tschumi's position at Downsview is symmetrical with his original thesis for Parc de la Villette. Both projects were based on a fundamental indictment of the 19th-century Olmstedian model, offering in its place an understanding of landscape as implicated in an effectively "planetary urbanization." As Tschumi put it in his project statement, "neither theme park or wildlife preserve, Downsview does not seek to renew using the conventions of traditional park compositions such as those of Vaux or Olmsted...Airstrips, information centers, public performance spaces, internet and worldwide web access all point to a redefinition of received ideas about parks, nature, and recreation, in a 21st-century setting where everything is 'urban,' even in the middle of the wilderness."[13]

Since the canonical case of Downsview, international design competitions have invited landscape and urbanism proposals for a host of redundant airport sites in cities around the world. Recent projects for airport conversions in Berlin (2012), Reykjavík (2013), Quito (2011), Caracas (2012), Casablanca (2007), and Taichung (2011) are indicative of this tendency. In each of these cases, the finalist projects collectively embodied the aspirations of landscape urbanist practice. Eelco Hooftman/GROSS.MAX.'s competition-winning project for the conversion of Berlin's Tempelhof Airport; Henri Bava/Agence Ter's proposal for Casablanca; Luis Callejas's schemes for Quito and Caracas; and Chris Reed/Stoss Landscape Urbanism's design for Taichung Gateway Park are notable evidence of the fecundity of landscape urbanist practices for the abandoned airfield.

While the redevelopment of abandoned airfields as large landscape projects is clearly relevant to the projective potentials of landscape urbanism, the much more challenging project is for the conception of the operational airfield as a landscape in its own right. The most comprehensive project in this regard is the master plan project for Amsterdam Airport Schiphol by Adriaan Geuze/West 8.[14]

West 8's ambitious scheme abandons the professional tradition of specifically detailed planting plans, deploying instead a general botanical strategy of sunflowers, clover, and beehives. This work, by avoiding intricate compositional designs and precise planting arrangements, allows the project to respond to future programmatic and political changes, positioning landscape as a strategic partner in the complex process of airport planning rather than (as is more often the case) simply an unfortunate victim of it. This positioning of the landscape medium as an open-ended and flexible matrix for future indeterminacy echoes Tschumi's arguments for both Parc de la Villette and Downsview, while reiterating one of the most often staked claims for landscape urbanism. Although runway alignments tend to be among the most durable of urban constructions, rarely if ever removed once built, the operational airfield, the airport itself, and the surrounding urban field face a virtually continual program of construction, demolition, and renovation. In the context of such malleability and flux, particularly one characterized by enormous horizontal fields of urbanization, landscape offers both medium and model for urban order.

13 Bernard Tschumi, "Downsview Park: The Digital and the Coyote," in CASE: Downsview Park Toronto, ed. Czerniak, 82–89.

14 See Adriaan Geuze/West 8, "West 8 Landscape Architects," in Het Landschap/The Landscape: Four International Landscape Designers (Antwerp: deSingel, 1995), 215–253; and Luca Molinari, ed., West 8 (Milan: Skira, 2000).

Airport Operations

From the beginning of the Jet Age, and since the 1990s in particular, operating airports increasingly have been perceived as landscape infrastructure. Landscape architects have seized the opportunity to design and plan the airport landscape on the land- and airsides. Airport authorities have realized that landscape management plans and landscape designs are necessary to mitigate air, soil, and water pollution, manage storm water and wildlife, and enhance the airport's aesthetic appearance.

Amsterdam Airport Schiphol connects to the larger landscape through gridded birch groves, new water canals, and retention basins. The landscape designs integrate wildlife management practices. The choice of plant species and the size of water bodies deter birds from feeding, nesting, and roosting near the airport. Munich Airport has used the site's historic field patterns and biotope structures in the airport's open-space designs and in the design of its storm-water management and water retention system. From the beginning, the airport was conceived as an iconic landscape that is both connected to and distinct from its surroundings. Oslo Airport is embedded in the local forest landscape, and the new landside landscape designs for Auckland Airport seek to foster an identity by using local agricultural patterns and planting features characteristic of indigenous and European settlers' cultures. In the 1990s, the city of Chicago explored the option of building Calumet Airport on brownfields in Southeast Chicago to alleviate traffic congestion at O'Hare. The project was also used as a catalyst for environmental remediation plans for this part of the city.

Landscape designs and certain landscape management strategies have sought to transform airport sites into more aesthetically pleasing and environmentally sensitive environments, while accommodating safe air traffic on large surfaces of asphalt and concrete. Landscape design and management at airports can both soften and emphasize the technological features and built structures, and remediate some of the adverse effects of aviation, for example, by managing and filtering storm-water runoff.

AMS

Amsterdam Airport Schiphol, The Netherlands. 1992; construction 1994–1998.
West 8 Urban Design & Landscape Architecture

Oblique aerial photo of the terminal area.

　　Airport Operations

The first airport near Amsterdam was built in 1916 on the Haarlemmermeer polder, a drained lakebed. Many ships capsized there in the early 1800s, giving the location the name "Schiphol," meaning "ship grave." Amsterdam Airport Schiphol (AMS) is located on the polder, six meters below sea level. Initially used by the military, Schiphol opened for commercial operation in 1920. As a result of expanding air traffic, in 1967 the airport was moved to its current location. It became one of the busiest airports in Europe, and by the late 1980s, a new master plan for expansion had been developed. An integral part of this plan was a practical, low-maintenance landscape strategy that was to respond to future growth and changing conditions while safeguarding the site's ecological integrity.

West 8 Urban Design & Landscape Architecture has been involved in the design and development of the landscape at AMS since 1993. The firm's key initiative was the preparation of a policy document that defined a set of objectives and principles for landscape design and management. These guidelines are now evident across the entire Schiphol area. West 8's director, Adriaan Geuze, continues to play a leading role as landscape supervisor, assuring adherence to the landscape standards. As the airport grows in size and complexity, subsequent policy documents and design manuals are being released and updated. West 8's ongoing involvement in urban and landscape initiatives varies in scale and type, and is increasingly focusing on the management of change, ensuring Schiphol's exemplary position in "green" and sustainable airport development.

West 8's planting and management concept for a "green airport" distinguishes three areas: the central area, a surrounding girdle of elm trees, and leftover spaces. In the central area, the firm proposed rough grassland along the runways and manicured lawn along the taxiways. The core of the airport is surrounded by a ring of elms—reminiscent of the elm avenues typical of the Dutch countryside—connecting green nodes planted with London plane trees. Leftover spaces outside of the runways are also planted in a way that creates a transparent vegetative veil or "green haze" that unifies the buildings and grounds of the expanded airport area. Viewsheds between runways, the terminal building, the radar station, and the lights had to be maintained to ensure the safe and smooth functioning of the airport. In the springtime, daffodils planted underneath the trees form geometrically shaped fields and add color, while clover was used as an initial groundcover to fertilize soils. By strategically placing beehives, clover could be naturally propagated until it was replaced in the natural succession by grass species. The airport was merged with the surrounding agricultural landscape by planting grids of 25,000 inexpensive native birch trees (*Betula pubescens*) that during the course of time would be thinned out and turned into wooded areas of varied density. Birch trees are not attractive to birds and can therefore help prevent collisions between birds and jets. To further contribute to the prevention of these collisions, all water bodies designed for storm-water drainage and retention comply with specified measurements that reduce the attraction of birds.

Plan of terminal area.

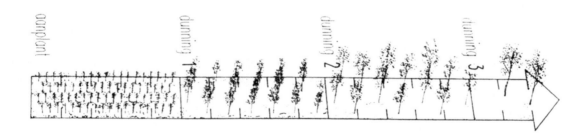

Diagram illustrating the planting strategy for birch groves.

Collage illustrating the birch groves, swaths of daffodils, and beehives.

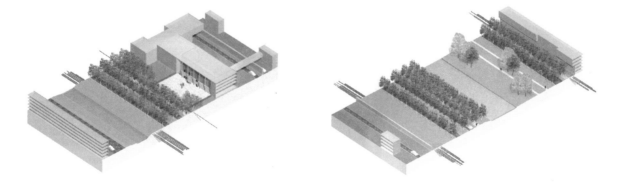

Axonometric drawings illustrating different profiles of landscape treatment throughout the site.

MUC

Munich Airport, Germany. 1976–1992.
Grünplan GmbH

Oblique aerial photograph looking east.

The new Munich Airport, located 28 kilometers northeast of the city, opened in 1992 after a planning process of 16 years. The decision to move the airport to the area called Erdinger Moos, a bog that was drained and cultivated in the 19th century, was made in 1969. The site's cultural and natural history was fundamental for the landscape plan and the comprehensive design framework for the airport, which was drawn up in the 1970s. The objective was to mitigate the environmental impact of the airport while creating an airport landscape with aesthetic appeal that could forge an identity for the new transportation hub. These early plans have been extended, determining the airport's role in the spatial configuration and landscape development of the entire region.

The landscape plans and design guidelines for the airport build on the site's existing landscape structure. The geometry and horizontality of the flat landscape, consisting of open fields and meadows, canals, and allées, have been incorporated in the design. The site's geometry follows a northeast-southwest orientation, and the north-south- and east-west-oriented airport structures have been overlaid to create both continuity throughout the larger landscape and an airport-specific landscape. A central allée forms the backbone of the entire airport, and other tree lines and gridded groves structure the open spaces in the terminal area. Site-specific tree and shrub species are planted to form a new landscape together with storm-water ditches, water-retention ponds, ramps, terraces, and other landforms, including the carefully graded viewing platforms surrounding the airport. A regional greenway running northeast to southwest connects the airport landscape to the regional open-space network. Parts of this greenway's diverse biotopes were created as environmental measures that compensated for airport construction.

Aerial and ground views of the airport landscape near the terminal area.

OSL

Oslo Airport, Gardermoen, Norway. 1989–1998.
Aviaplan Architects, Engineers, and Landscape Architects
Bjørbekk & Lindheim AS
13.3 Landscape Architects

Oblique aerial view of design, 1993.

The new international airport near Oslo opened in 1998 and covers an area of 13.5 square kilometers. The design embeds the airport into a coniferous forest, with short paths between the "forest car park" and the terminal building. Allées of birch trees and plantings of other deciduous trees structure the landscape on the airport landside. The planners and designers who developed a design handbook with ideas and concepts to be followed in the airport development established the premise of close ties between the airport and the natural landscape surrounding it. Overall, the airport is intended to express a Norwegian vernacular. The forest reaches right up to the terminal building. Emphasis was placed on the use of local materials and resources in the airport buildings.

Recent plans for a terminal expansion have been drawn up for an incremental growth of up to 36 million passengers per year, with an annual capacity of approximately 17 million passengers in the first phase. These plans make sure that all functional areas can be expanded without affecting neighboring areas or compromising the main "airport forest" concept. Moreover, the airside taxiway system is designed to minimize aircraft movements on the ground.

Views of the airport and the "airport forest."

AKL

Auckland Airport, Auckland, New Zealand. Commenced 2007.
Surfacedesign, Inc.

Detail of first landing site and stone water-management
system of the larger landscape. Water runoff is treated and
released back into the creek.

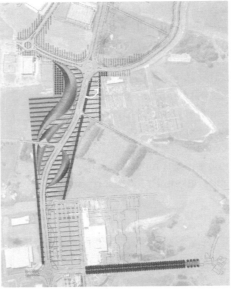

Earth-formed blades and hedgerows recalling the Maori
stone field and early European settlements.

Section showing a transect through the native New Zealand landscape. The planting
scheme used at the Auckland Airport allows visitors to experience the types of vegetation
that grow in different parts of the island.

Since 2007, Auckland International Airport Limited (AIAL) and the Auckland City Council have collaborated with the firm Surfacedesign on a comprehensive landscape and urban design vision for future development at the airport. The AIAL board and its property division recognize that landscape will be critical to ensure the value of its property holdings by creating a memorable connection to New Zealand for its tenants, employees, and visitors. Surfacedesign's master plan includes a sculpture park, a training facility for professional rugby, a linear park and streetscape extending over three kilometers beginning at the airport entrance, and a park that encompasses the restoration of an important Maori Marae and European homestead.

In its designs for the landside areas of the airport, Surfacedesign has used local plants and vernacular forms common to the cultivated landscapes of New Zealand. Remnants of ancient Maori settlements and hedgerows planted by early farmers are seen throughout the airport site. These elements serve as a reminder of the adversities that early settlers faced on arrival to New

Zealand. To create the microclimates necessary to sustain their settlements, the Maori communities utilized extinct volcanic cones and built shell middens to protect the tropical crops they brought from Polynesia. European settlers took advantage of the stands of native bush, combining it with poplar and eucalyptus hedgerows to create protected plots for growing food. By using these and other local characteristics in the airport landscape, the designs seek to foster an identity that helps to connect air travelers to New Zealand.

CALUMET

Lake Calumet Airport and Southeast Chicago Environmental Plan. 1990–1992.
City of Chicago, Office of Mayor Richard M. Daley

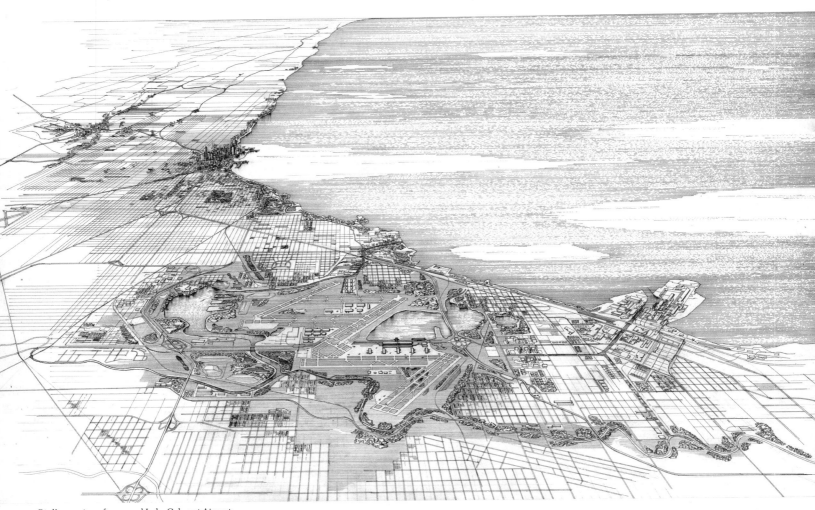

Bird's-eye view of proposed Lake Calumet Airport.

CALUMET

The Lake Calumet Airport project was a proposal for a major new airport to alleviate plane traffic congestion at O'Hare International Airport. It was developed by the City of Chicago from 1990 to 1992. Planned for a brownfield site in Southeast Chicago, it was put forward as an alternative to the greenfield development proposals. The controversial project was intended to address the consequence of 100 years of unsupervised development on the city's southeast side.

The city adopted a comprehensive environmental plan that crossed state boundaries and was included in the early stages of airport development. The project also promoted industrial and multimodal development, the revitalization

of the international freight harbor, and the restructuring of landfills. Although the project was not implemented, it focused the city's attention on preserving natural assets in the Calumet region by developing infrastructure projects on brownfield rather than greenfield sites. The Lake Calumet Airport Proposal and the Southeast Chicago Environmental Plan both won awards from Progressive Architecture's New Public Realm Competition.

Plan showing different landscape categories.

Diagrams illustrating existing conditions and projected transformations.

Airport Operations

Various plant and animal species have been used
in the management of airport landscapes,
including peregrine falcons, sheep, and llamas,
as well as genetically engineered fescue cultivars.
The animals' grazing habits and the wildlife
and habitat management strategies that involve
grass species selection can be used instead of
other technologies like sound cannons to scare
away birds.

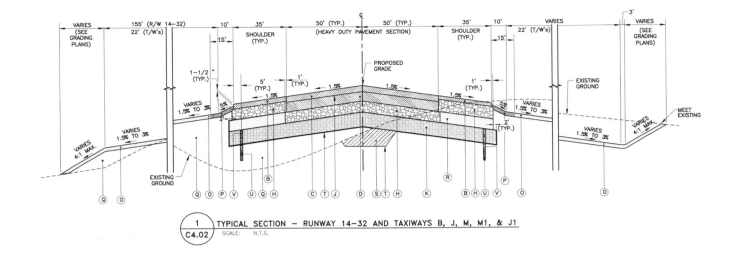

1 / TYPICAL SECTION – RUNWAY 14–32 AND TAXIWAYS B, J, M, M1, & J1
C4.02 SCALE: N.T.S.

Runway Section

Airport runways (where aircraft land and take off), taxiways (where aircraft taxi to and from runways to gates and parking positions), and apron areas (contact gates at terminals or remote parking) are often constructed using hot mix asphalt or Portland cement concrete. Hot mix asphalt is more flexible, but also less durable. Cement is used on many heavy-duty runways, intensely used runway areas, and airfield aprons. Airports in warmer climates often depend more on concrete than other materials. Pavement core samples are taken to determine the structural integrity of existing pavement, and are taken during construction to test and ensure that the applied pavement meets the required density, stability, and air void requirements.

The hot mix asphalt is composed of asphalt cement (also known as asphalt binder), well-graded aggregates ranging from sand to material 2.5 to 3.8 centimeters in size, and if needed, a mineral filler. The asphalt is a dark brown to black material that consists of bitumen, a hydrocarbon that is a product of petroleum processing. The asphalt binder is a thick, sticky, viscoelastic material that acts as a bonding agent with the aggregates and mineral filler when heated during the production of hot mix asphalt. This mixture is thoroughly compacted when placed. When cooled, the bond between the asphalt, aggregates, and mineral filler bind together to form hot mix asphalt pavement. At Boston Logan International Airport, hot mix asphalt averages approximately

33 centimeters in depth, with some areas close to a depth of 61 centimeters.

Portland cement concrete (PCC) is used on aircraft parking aprons and select taxiways at Logan International Airport. The concrete is used in areas subjected to static loads and in areas where aircraft may be fueled, particularly in terminal apron areas. The taxiways that have PCC at Logan are heavy traffic areas where aircraft are often asked to wait to cross another pavement or enter a runway. A typical PCC pavement section at Logan consists of 15 inches of PCC on top of a granular base course. The PCC is comprised of cement, well-graded aggregate ranging from sand to material 2.5 to 3.8 centimeters in size, fly ash, and admixtures needed to entrain air or reduce the water of the PCC. The PCC pavement at Logan is also reinforced with welded wire fabric and dowels between the placed slabs.

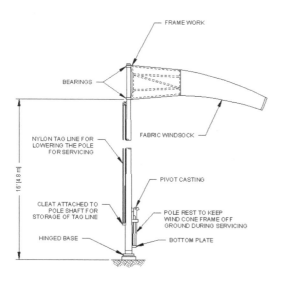

FRAME WORK

BEARINGS

FABRIC WINDSOCK

NYLON TAG LINE FOR
LOWERING THE POLE
FOR SERVICING

PIVOT CASTING

16' [4.8 m]

CLEAT ATTACHED TO
POLE SHAFT FOR
STORAGE OF TAG LINE

POLE REST TO KEEP
WIND CONE FRAME OFF
GROUND DURING SERVICING

HINGED BASE

BOTTOM PLATE

Windsock

This windsock meets the requirements of the US Federal Aviation Administration (FAA). Windsocks at airports are up to 3.75 meters long and measure up to 0.9 meters in diameter. The taper of the fabric windsock from the throat to the trailing end is designed to cause the windsock to fully extend when exposed to a wind of 28 kilometers per hour. A framework is provided to hold the throat of the fabric windsock fully open even under conditions of no wind. The framework also needs to maintain the windsock in a rigid position for three-eighths of its length. Together with its framework, the windsock performs as a wind vane. The structure is designed to move freely about the vertical shaft to which it is attached when subjected to winds of 5.6 kilometers per hour or more. It indicates the true wind direction within five degrees. The color of windsocks can be orange, white, orange and white, or red and white stripes. Colors are selected to make the windsocks sufficiently visible against their respective backgrounds.

Eelgrass and Terns

San Diego International Airport (SAN), located in species-rich San Diego Bay, has developed a protected nesting site for the California least tern, an endangered migrating seabird that nests in the region's tidelands before heading south during the winter. The protected fenced-off nesting grounds are located on sand and gravel between the runway and taxiways. The airport closely monitors nesting activities and works to keep predators at bay. In the protected areas, all airport activities are prohibited, vehicle speed is reduced to 25 kilometers per hour, and lights needed for construction projects at night have to be turned away. As a result of these measures, SAN boasts one of the highest percentages of surviving tern fledglings in the region.

To improve the habitat of the nesting terns the airport has also sought to minimize the impacts of stormwater runoff on the eelgrass beds that grow in the San Diego Bay area. They are an important foraging ground for the terns.

Goats

Domestic goats graze fields at the San Francisco Airport (SFO), SeaTac Airport (SEA) in Seattle, Chicago O'Hare International Airport (ORD), and Bend Municipal Airport (BDN) in Oregon. The airports have turned to goats as an environmentally sustainable method for managing plant populations on their grounds. Each spring, SFO has to create a firebreak to protect nearby houses during the dry season without harming the San Francisco garter snake and the California red-legged frog—two endangered species that inhabit the area. For the past five years, the airport has replaced noisy weed-whackers with a herd of 400 goats that graze away a six-meter buffer along its western edge, working efficiently while leaving the endangered species undisturbed. SEA, ORD, BDN, and others have also adopted what is known as "prescribed grazing," replacing toxic chemicals and heavy machinery with the nimble, voracious animals to control invasive brush and weeds. Recently ORD added a herd of goats to its sheep, llamas, and donkeys as part of an ongoing effort to reduce its carbon footprint.

Llamas

The financial and environmental costs to maintain large airport grounds using heavy machinery and human labor are considerable. In an effort to curb these costs and become more environmentally sustainable, Chicago O'Hare International Airport (ORD) and Hartsfield-Jackson Atlanta International Airport (ATL) are using grazers—including donkeys, llamas, and sheep—that munch away at problem areas each season. At ORD, these species clear weeds and brush in places that not even the most sophisticated machines could reach, eliminating invasive plants and depleting food supplies for geese and other potentially hazardous birds. They also crop long grass that is the breeding ground for small rodents that attract birds of prey, who in turn can collide with aircraft. Both airports have found this method to be cost-efficient and environmentally sustainable, as it reduces fuel emissions and harmful chemicals.

Coyote Decoy

While fences may keep deer and larger wildlife away from airport runways, they cannot keep small animals and birds from entering the airport from the air. At some airports, including Kalamazoo / Battle Creek International Airport (AZO), employees decided to try using coyotes as a scare tactic, but the four seen lurking around its runways are only decoys. Airport employees move the plastic model predators, each one given a different name, to new locations each day. The decoys are not identical, and some are positioned so that they move slightly with the wind. AZO's band of "coyotes" look convincing enough to keep geese and other wildlife at bay. Decoys like these are also used to deter geese, ducks, rabbits, and rodents from golf courses, large estates, parks, and other grass and turf areas where these animals are not desired.

Peregrine Falcon

John F. Kennedy International Airport in New York City has been the only commercial airport in the United States to use falconry, a common wildlife management practice at European airports, to scare away birds such as gulls, geese, starlings, pigeons, and doves. "Bird strike" and "bird ingestion" (the collision of aircraft and birds) present a danger at airports that can lead to fatal accidents and aircraft damage. Airports are often the only large open areas with grassland in otherwise densely built-up urban agglomerations, and therefore attract many bird species for nesting and roosting. The peregrine falcon is a predator that feeds on medium-sized birds such as waterfowl, pigeons, doves, songbirds, and waders. Falcons flying near airports and in their boundary zones scare away and significantly reduce the number of these birds, contributing to the prevention of collisions between aircraft and birds. Airport falconers drive around the airport accompanied by the falcon in the air. The mere presence of the flying falcon scares away many of its prey. Peregrine falcons are renowned for their speed and high-speed hunting dives, reaching over 322 kilometers per hour. In comparison, a typical cruise speed of the Boeing 747 at an altitude of 10.6 kilometers is 913 kilometers per hour.

The stuffed peregrine falcon in this image hatched in 1877, several decades before the invention of powered flight. The Museum of Comparative Zoology, Department of Ornithology, at Harvard University acquired it in 1910. In 1961, the Museum advised and assisted the Massachusetts Port Authority in its effort to prevent future bird strikes after the crash of an Eastern Airlines Lockheed Electra aircraft at Boston Logan International Airport in October 1960, due to its collision with a flock of starlings. Discussions at the time included the proposal to learn from falconry practices at European airports.

RoBird

As the number of bird strikes has increased over the past decade, so too have attempts to curb them. These efforts range from firearms and sound cannons to live falcons and a variety of landscape management practices. Most of these methods can only temporarily disperse hazardous birds, rather than permanently keep them away from airport territories. To address this problem, researchers are turning to robotics. The RoBird, a robotic peregrine falcon designed to scare away birds from airports, flaps its wings in a lifelike imitation of a raptor's attack behavior. It is very robust and can fly in winds of up to 5 Bft (11 meters/second, 21 knots), with its fastest speed at 75 kilometers per hour. The remotely piloted machine relies on birds' instinctive fear of raptors. The robot can be deployed quickly, responding to changing conditions and aircraft traffic patterns. RoBird is still only a prototype being tested for use at operating airports.

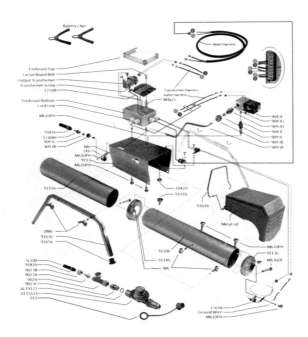

Sound Cannon

A number of wildlife management practices are used at airports to prevent collisions between aircraft and wildlife. In most cases, multiple practices are used simultaneously. To scare away birds, many airports deploy sound cannons, including the propane-powered sound cannon used at Boston Logan International Airport. The sound cannon provides a single-pressure regulated blast to frighten and disorient birds. At Logan, several sound cannons are located near the airport boundary. They can be fired and controlled remotely, enabling a flexible reaction to bird movement around the airport.

Sound cannons are among sonic dispersal techniques at airports that include shell crackers and pyrotechnics. They are particularly effective in scaring away migratory bird species. Sound cannons can complement other management practices to scare off birds, including falconry, habitat modification, and the management of land use surrounding the airport. Barriers such as fences and netting are used to restrict and control the movement of mammals. Trapping, shooting, and poisoning are also employed to prevent collisions between aircraft and wildlife.

At some American and European airports, a concerted effort has been made to avoid sonic and chemical devices, and instead to focus on landscape management practices, which require a detailed analysis of airport ecology. Depending on the bird species that pose the hazard, management practices such as the cultivation of extensive meadows instead of cropped lawns and the replacement of agricultural fields with shrubbery and young forests have been used to decrease the threat of bird strikes.

Tall Fescue Grass

Avian collisions with aircraft, known as "bird strikes," are becoming increasingly common and cost the global airline industry an estimated $1.5 billion each year. Collisions between birds and planes can cause expensive structural damage to aircraft and may lead to crashes and emergency landings (including the storied Hudson River landing in 2009). Strategic tall fescue grass plantings can render airports less appealing as feeding, breeding, and resting zones for birds.

John F. Kennedy International Airport is exploring the cultivation of tall fescue grass as a deterrent to waterfowl and migratory birds. The hardy, dense perennial grass sometimes houses a fungal endophyte (*Neotyphodium coenophialum*) that birds dislike eating. Its height also makes this grass less attractive to geese and other migratory species that prefer to feed on low-growing grassland. Located near the Jamaica Bay Wildlife Refuge, JFK is an area rich with Kentucky bluegrass that "is like candy to the geese." The airport has emphasized this kind of grass management as part of its broader strike-reduction plan.

Given the natural potential of tall fescue grass to mitigate bird strikes at airports, researchers are exploring how to turn it into an even stronger deterrent. Scientists in New Zealand have trademarked a new grass seed engineered to contain a fungal endophyte. This fungus, which doesn't affect the grass's growth or appearance, produces a toxin that makes geese and other grazing birds lethargic and sick. It also deters insects that are another food source for the birds. While researchers maintain that this "jackal-like" tall fescue grass does not permanently harm grazing birds, it effectively repels them. At several New Zealand airports where the grass has been used, bird populations have significantly shrunk and the number of bird strikes has dropped between 70 and 90 percent.

Airport Photography

Andreas Gursky
Vera Lutter
Hubert Blanz
Richard Mosse
Jeffrey Milstein
Alex MacLean
Yann Arthus-Bertrand
Robert Burley
Kathleen Shafer
Phil Underdown

Since the 1990s, airfields and airports have increasingly attracted the attention of fine art photographers. The work of the 10 photographers featured here presents the airport as an infrastructure situated in a field of tension—an artificial, precisely engineered, and strictly controlled environment that is equally subject to human failure and the uncontrollable forces of non-human nature.

Andreas Gursky's photographs of the Schiphol and Düsseldorf airports appear to capture the airport as non-place, as theorized by Marc Augé. On the vast expanse of the field, framed by the slick modernist architecture of terminal buildings, humans are out of place, lost in a hyper-technological environment. The airport is a void characterized by a distinct lack of place—in many ways it is a locale that is off-limits. As other photographs in Gursky's airport series show, the airside can be inhabited only on special occasions.

In her black-and-white photographs of hangars at Lemwerder and aircraft at Frankfurt Airport, Vera Lutter evokes the uncanny. Taken with exposures of several hours or days, the aircraft appear as mystical machines with lives of their own. Our common apprehension and anticipation of flight, and the freedom and speed often associated with it, are questioned in these photographs that draw attention to the dark and secretive side of technology. Even more explicit is the disorientation created by the photographic collages of Hubert Blanz. He assembles vertical and oblique aerial photographs of runways from various airports, cropped from aerial photographs retrieved from the Internet. Labyrinthine layers of airstrips running in all directions plaster the entire picture. Richard Mosse also questions the power of flight, but unlike Vera Lutter, he highlights its danger and terror, seeking to visually represent disaster. In his series "Airside," he presents the eerie and alienating atmosphere of isolated dummy airplanes used at airports to practice extinguishing aircraft fires and rescuing passengers. In another series, "The Fall," Mosse offers images of crashed airplanes in remote areas across the globe, anticipating how they will slowly disintegrate as they merge with the surrounding nature.

In contrast to both Mosse and Lutter, Jeffrey Milstein presents the power and elegance of the flying machine in his series "Aircraft." Showing aircraft from below and in descent from the front, Milstein isolates the planes from their background, thus making them appear as technologically pristine machines. In his series "Flying Over Airports," Milstein's aerial views emphasize the long shadows toward the end of the day, and the illumination at night, making airports appear as they are—inhabited, lively transportation hubs.

In Alex MacLean's aerial airport photographs, airport runways become abstract patterns. His photographs highlight the surface structure, texture, and colors, and render the airport as a distanced and disembodied infrastructure of precision. Yann Arthus-Bertrand zooms into airport runways even further. The detailed photographs of his "Tarmac" series create a new type of aerial archaeology that reveals layers of runway markings, skid marks, and rubber wheel traces from the landing planes and reduces them to abstract patterns.

The juxtaposition of technology and landscape along the edges of operating airports and on closed airfields is the theme in photographs by Robert Burley, Kathleen Shafer, and Phil Underdown. Burley explores the vegetation and wildlife along airport edges, while Shafer has experimented with various ways of depicting both the scale and the stillness of smaller operating airports and decommissioned fields such as Berlin Tempelhof Airport. Underdown's atmospheric landscape photography of his "Grassland" series highlights the ephemeral character of both human-made infrastructure and non-human nature by capturing an abandoned airstrip in today's Shawangunk Grasslands National Wildlife Refuge in New York State.

Andreas Gursky
Düsseldorf, Flughafen II, 1994

Andreas Gursky
Schiphol, 1994

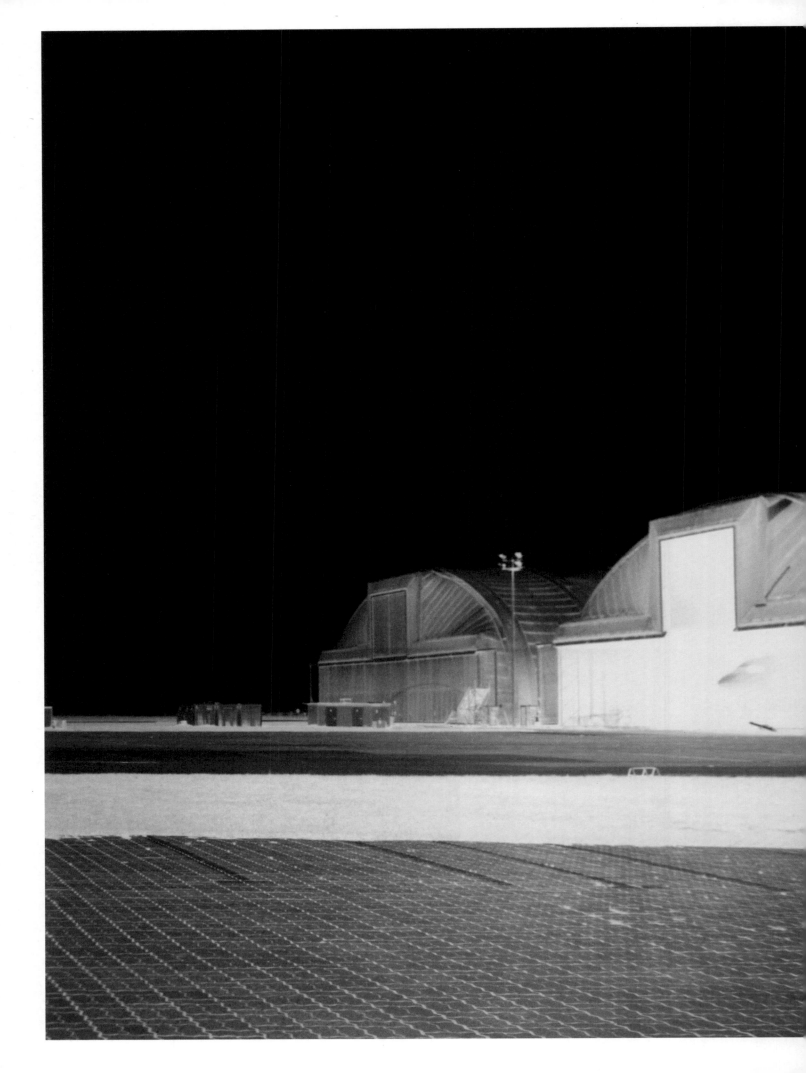

Vera Lutter
Airplane with Ghost, Lemwerder: August 15, 1997

Vera Lutter
Frankfurt Airport, VII: April 24, 2001

Hubert Blanz
X-Plantation, 05, 2008

Hubert Blanz
X-Plantation, 06, 2008

Richard Mosse
A320 Blackpool, 2008

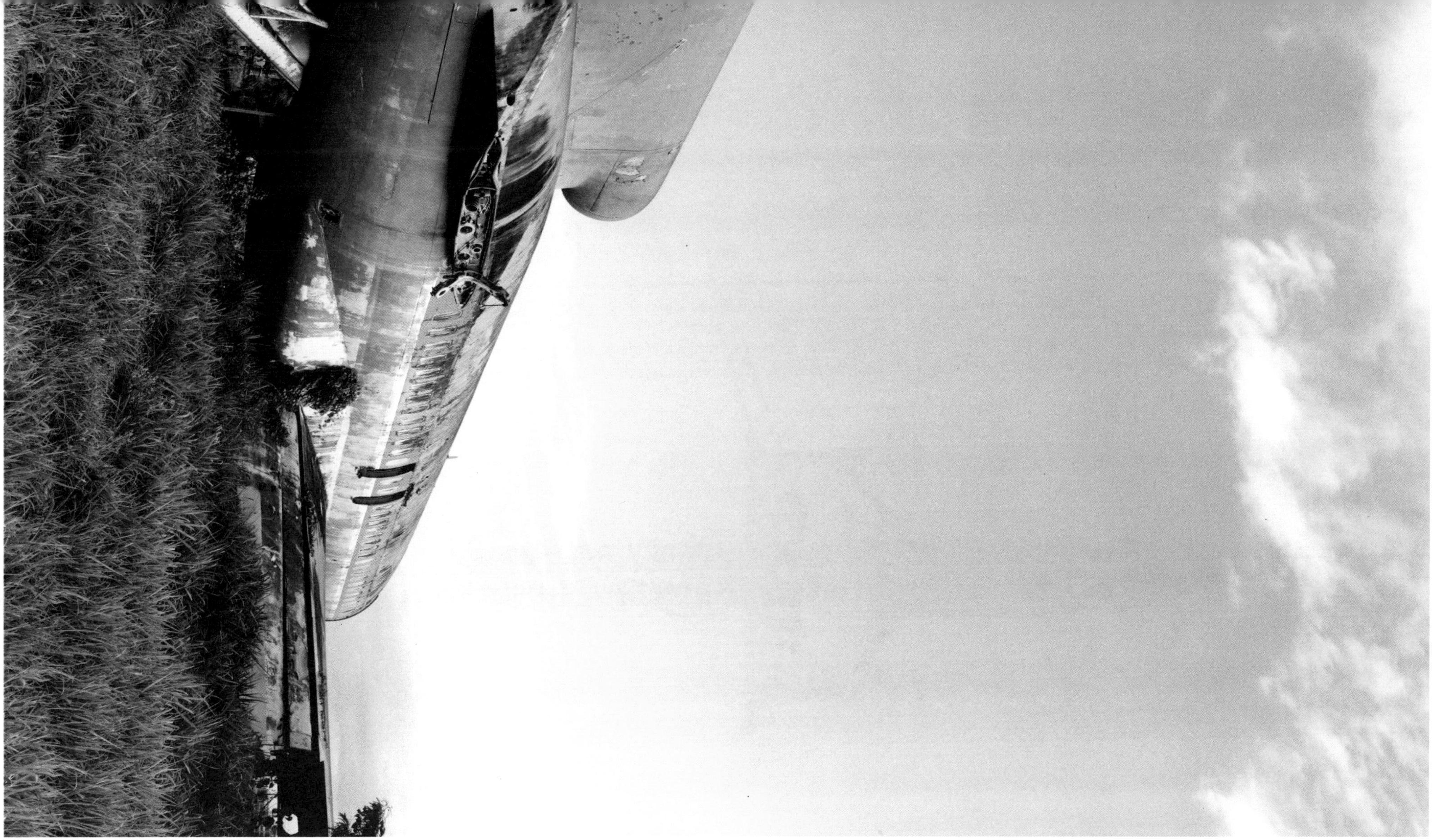

Richard Mosse
The Fall 727 *Santo Domingo, January* 2009

Jeffrey Milstein
Alaska Airlines (Disneyland) Boeing 737-400, 2006

Jeffrey Milstein
Southwest Boeing 737-700, 2006

Jeffrey Milstein
JFK 01, 2013

Jeffrey Milstein
Newark 1, 2012

Alex MacLean
Runway, Omaha, NE, 2008

Alex MacLean
Runway, 2009

Alex MacLean
On Roll, Newark, NJ, 2010

Yann Arthus-Bertrand

Tarmac 2 – Aéroport de Paris-Roissy Charles de Gaulle, France, June 2007

Yann Arthus-Bertrand

Tarmac 3–Aéroport de Paris-Roissy Charles de Gaulle, France, June 2007

Yann Arthus-Bertrand
Tarmac 7—Aérport de Montevideo, Uruguay, January 2007

Yann Arthus-Bertrand
Tarmac 14–Aéroport de Paris-Roissy Charles de Gaulle, France, June 2007

Robert Burley
O'Hare Queen Anne's Lace, 1985

Robert Burley
O'Hare Animal Tracks, 1985

Robert Burley
O'Hare Spring Flowers, 1986

Robert Burley
O'Hare Radio Towers, 1988

Kathleen Shafer
Untitled (Tempelhof, Hangar), 2011

Kathleen Shafer

X, 2010

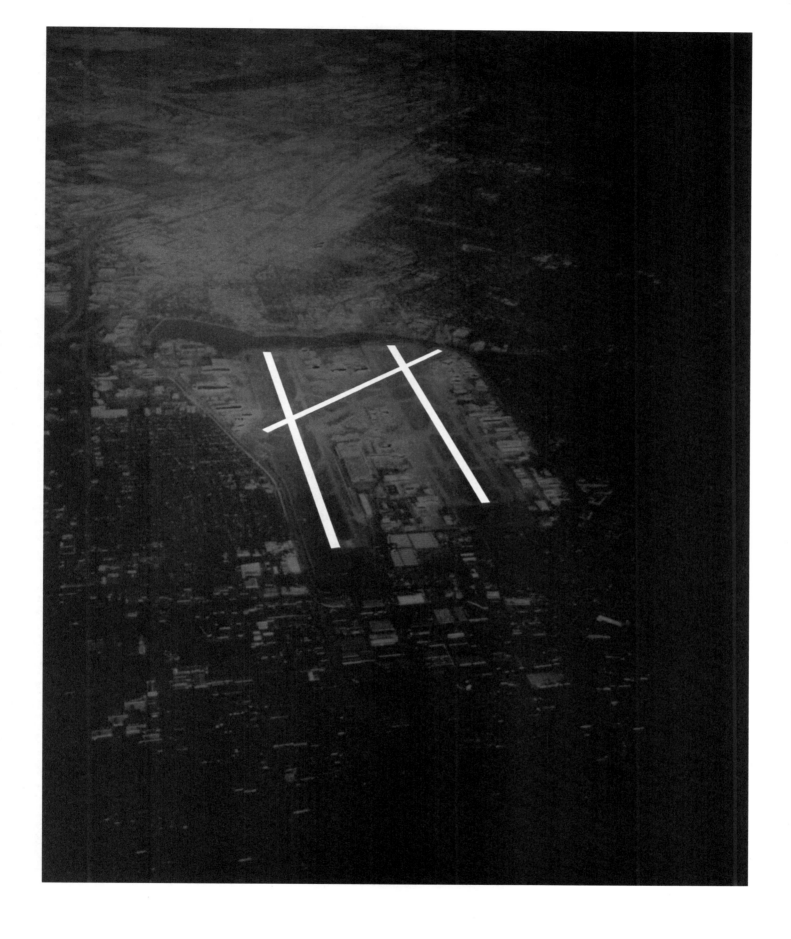

Kathleen Shafer
Shift A, 2009

Kathleen Shafer
Hangar (HAF), 2006

Kathleen Shafer
Runway (HAF), 2006

Phil Underdown
Grassland #110, 2004

Phil Underdown
Grassland #038, 2005

Phil Underdown
Grassland #204, 2006

Phil Underdown
Grassland #394, 2006

A large lava rock fountain illuminated by colored lights at night was constructed at the main entrance to Honolulu International Airport in 1964.

Airport, Landscape, Environment

Airport, Landscape, Environment

Sonja Dümpelmann

Someone needs to invent new airports.
—Senator A. S. Mike Monroney (aka "Mr. Aviation"), 1969

By the late 1960s, many leading cultural, architecture, and landscape critics in the United States had characterized the airport and its environment as a dystopia—the opposite of a pleasurable landscape, even an anti-landscape. Landscape architect Ian McHarg spoke for many when he commented that "airports are places one would rather avoid," observing that aviation had been preoccupied with speed rather than quality of experience.[1] He criticized the neglect of nature in airport design, arguing for his method of "creative fitting" and for ecological planning as a tool for aviation planning.[2]

Historian and cultural commentator Lewis Mumford was perhaps most critical about the visual and cultural aspect of the airport landscape, which appeared to him as a wasteland. He explained in dry, ironic prose that the words park and field "have taken on new meanings" when considering the airport. "Park" now meant a "desert of asphalt, designed as a temporary storage space for motor cars," whereas "field" referred to "another kind of artificial desert, a barren area planted in great concrete strips, vibrating with noise, dedicated to the arrival and departure of planes." Mumford felt that parking lots and airports grew "at the expense of parkland around every big city." If this development continued, he argued, the result would be a "universal paved desert, unfit for human

1   Ian McHarg, "Ecological Planning for Evolutionary Success," in *Master Planning the Aviation Environment*, ed. Angelo J. Cerchione, Victor E. Rothe, and James Vercellino (Tuscon, AZ: University of Arizona Press, 1969), 7–10 (7).

2   Ibid.

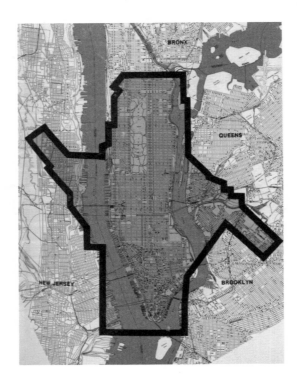

habitation, no better than the surface of the moon."[3]

Boeing's launch of the 707 airliner in 1958 had marked the advent of the Jet Age that required new airports of unprecedented size.[4] The total apron area necessary for aircraft doubled between 1950 and 1960 and increased further in the following decade. The Boeing 707 needed an average apron area of 2,600 square meters, and the Boeing 747 first used by commercial airlines in 1970 required double that area. Dulles International Airport was built between 1958 and 1962 on a 4,000-hectare site as large as two-thirds of Manhattan Island, while 10 years later, Dallas/Fort Worth International Airport was constructed on a 7,122-hectare site that by far surpassed the size of Manhattan. Space and

design considerations did not relate only to the immediate airport area; the space surrounding airport boundaries was affected as well. Since the dawn of commercial flight, flight paths for takeoff and landing have led to height restrictions for nearby buildings, and aircraft have caused noise and air pollution, particularly along flight paths.

In the 1960s, it appeared as if aviation technology and its culture and environment were out of sync. Aviation engineer H. McKinley Conway, Jr. put it succinctly in 1968: "Despite the spectacular advances in aircraft design, we are still operating in a horse-and-buggy environment."[5] Acting Federal Aviation (FAA) administrator D. D. Thomas elaborated that the problem was one of "adjusting to 'horse and buggy' speeds,

3   Lewis Mumford, "The Social Function of Open Spaces," in Space for Living: Landscape Architecture and the Allied Arts and Professions, ed. Silvia Crowe (Amsterdam: Djambatan, 1961), 24, 26 (22–37); Lewis Mumford, "Die soziale Funktion der Freiräume," Baumeister 58 (April 1960): 322–328 (324, 328).

4   See Oscar Bakke, "The Aviation World of Tomorrow," in Master Planning the Aviation Environment, ed. Cerchione, et al., 3–5 (4).

5   H. McKinley Conway, Jr., "Crisis in Airport Planning," AirportWorld 1, no. 2 (1968): 50–53 (50).

Uprooting trees for the construction of Dulles International Airport, Chantilly, Virginia, between 1958 and 1962.

Construction of Dulles International Airport, Chantilly, Virginia, between 1958 and 1962.

once you get out of the jet airplane"—with contemporary traffic moving through the congested city at approximately six miles per hour, even more slowly than the 11 miles per hour of horse-drawn vehicles.[6] Architecture critic Reyner Banham described airports as transportation nodes that were already obsolete the moment they were inaugurated.[7] Architect Paolo Soleri criticized the airport as a "parasite appendix" of the city.[8] He proposed to turn the city into an air terminal, or the air terminal into a city—an idea that has been carried out by many airport authorities. Similarly, H. McKinley Conway, Jr., argued that, "the plan for a major new airport is nothing less than the plan for a 'new town' . . . for the city of tomorrow."[9]

The 1960s also marked a moment when the airport was considered both a landscape—a setting with scenic potential that required design and improvement—and an environment formed by natural processes and ecological systems. In the wake of the environmental movement, for some grassroots initiatives the airport even became the grounds for social utopias. The airport was not, in other words, considered by all to be the "non-place" later theorized by Marc Augé.[10] Since the beginning of commercial flight, significant efforts have been undertaken to turn airports into places, landscapes, and environments that can be safely and even pleasurably inhabited, if only for a transitory moment.

6   D. D. Thomas quoted in Chester A. Church, "Master-planning of Airspace: We're All Named George," in *Master Planning of Airspace: A Total Systems Approach*, proceedings of conference sponsored by the Arizona Department of Aeronautics, Arizona State University and Luke Air Force Base (1968): 52–65 (67).

7   Reyner Banham, "The Obsolescent Airport," *The Architectural Review* 788 (1962), 252–253.

8   Paolo Soleri, "The City as the Airport," in *Master Planning the Aviation Environment*, ed. Cerchione, et al., 11–13.

9   Conway, Jr., "Crisis," 50.

10   Marc Augé, *Non-Places: Introduction to an Anthropology of Supermodernity* (London and New York: Verso, 1995), 77–78.

Like McHarg, many in the 1960s criticized airports for their inhospitality. The psychologist Robert Sommer launched an attack on airport designers and authorities, writing that, "airport waiting areas are probably the most antisocial public spaces in America today."[11] Barbara DeBevoise, editor of the interior and architectural design journal *The Designer*, complained about airports' "impersonal design" and the fact that passengers were driven "from the free public [terminal] areas by making such areas unattractive and uncongenial."[12] So although the airport was seen by some as an engine of economic growth that could keep the faltering American city alive, it was also widely perceived as an ugly and purely functional site that passengers were forced to move through when traveling by air.[13]

The construction of the first jet airport outside of the US national capital, in Chantilly, Virginia, was an opportunity to draw attention to the design and planning opportunities inherent in this new type of infrastructure. Dulles International Airport was considered a model for the burgeoning Jet Age. The new scale of aviation had to be accommodated and further expansion anticipated. The preparation of the 4,000-hectare site required the removal or demolition of more than 300 buildings and farmsteads and the excavation of more than nine million cubic meters of earth. A construction progress report described the gargantuan task: "Huge bulldozers devoured the hedgerows. Hummocks were leveled, valleys filled, immense trenches opened and closed again over thousands of feet of drain pipe and electrical conduits. A mixing plant was erected and enormous quantities of materials were shipped in to manufacture concrete—250,000 tons of sand, 600,000 tons of crushed stone, and 750,000 barrels of cement."[14]

In addition to being conceived of as a huge infrastructural work of nearly unprecedented scale and as a functional air terminal, Dulles was to become a center of culture and beauty. Under the leadership of Elwood Richard Quesada, the FAA's first administrator (1959–1961), the project's principal contractor, the engineering firm Ammann and Whitney, commissioned Eero Saarinen's architecture firm as the lead designer. Eero Saarinen and Associates in turn soon involved landscape architect Daniel U. Kiley to consult on the airport landscape.

Kiley thereby came to collaborate on one of the most prestigious airport projects at the time, and he continued to work on airports throughout his career, including Kansai airport in Japan in the 1980s and a comprehensive—albeit only in small parts realized—landscape design for Dallas/Fort Worth International Airport in the late 1960s.[15] In the early 1960s, when the FAA turned to I. M. Pei & Associates for the design of a new prototypical freestanding air-traffic control tower, Kiley consulted on the surrounding grading and open-space design in multiple locations, including White Plains, New York; Lambert Field in St. Louis, Missouri; Columbia, South Carolina; and Andrews Air Force Base, Maryland. The architects had decided to locate all functions that did not require aerial and airfield vision in a submerged building at the base of the tower. With Kiley's help, the tower and its

---

11   Robert Sommer, "The Lonely Airport Crowd," *Airtravel* (1969): 16–22 (16).

12   Barbara DeBevoise, "Man is the Constant—Technology the Variable," in *Master Planning the Aviation Environment*, ed. Cerchione, et al., 139–143 (142–143).

13   Bakke, "Aviation World," 5.

14   Federal Aviation Agency, *Dulles International Airport, Construction Progress Report* (Washington, DC: Government Printing Office), 5–6.

15   For Kiley's work on the Dallas/Fort Worth International Airport, see Sonja Dümpelmann, "Der Flughafen als Landschaft," in *Ökologie und die Künste*, ed. Daniela Hahn and Erika Fischer-Lichte (Munich: Wilhelm Fink Verlag, 2015), 71–92; Dümpelmann, "The Landscapes of Airport Transfer," in *Thinking the Contemporary Landscape. Concepts and Methods*, ed. Christophe Girot and Dora Imhoff (New York: Princeton Architectural Press, 2016); and the exhibition "The Jetport Landscape," curated by the author and on display in the Frances Loeb Library of the Harvard University Graduate School of Design, Cambridge, Massachusetts, October 31, 2013–December 19, 2013.

Daniel Kiley, grading plan and landscape design for the air traffic control tower at Columbia, South Carolina, early 1960s.

Daniel Kiley, planting plan for Dulles International Airport, undated.

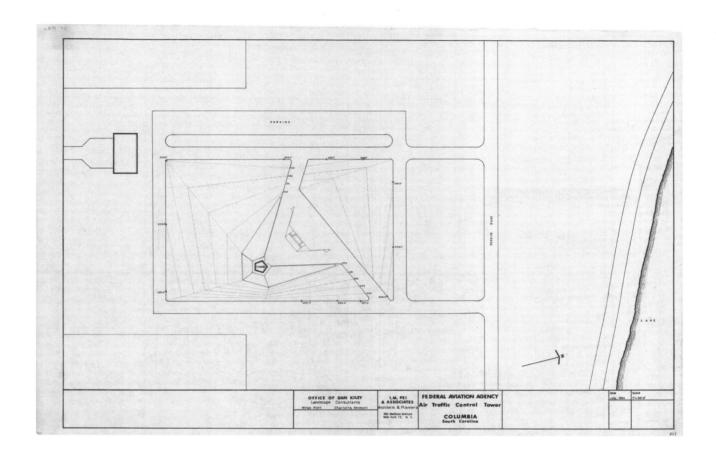

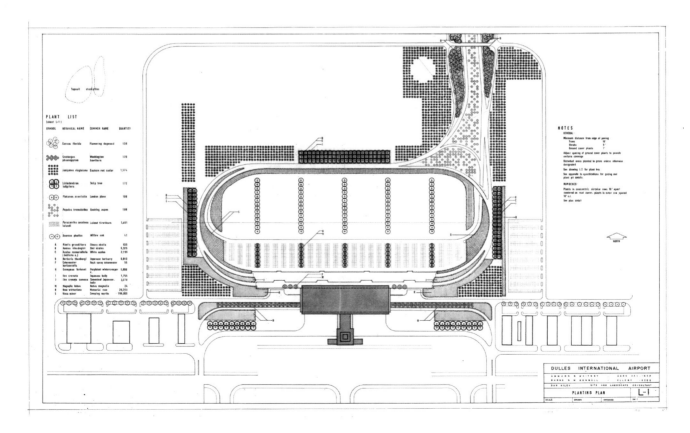

Terminal Area Zoning Plan showing Daniel Kiley's
landscape layout surrounding the terminal building and
the lake, Dulles International Airport, 1969.

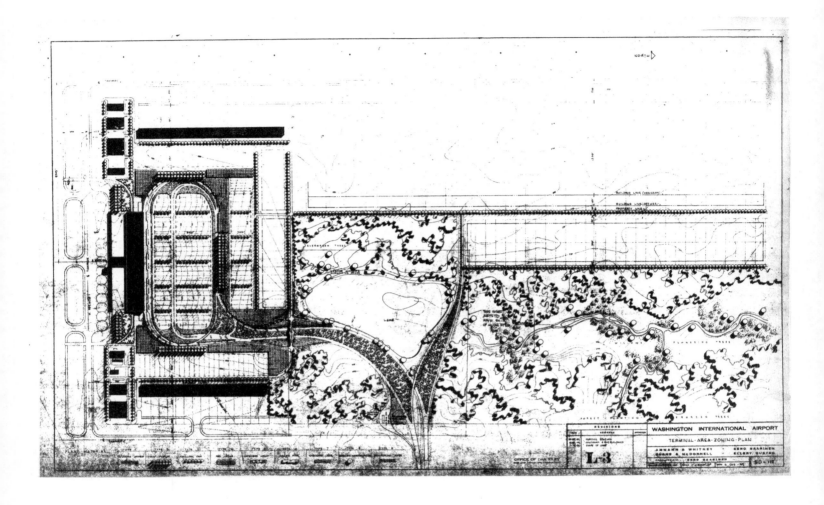

base building could easily be embedded in a sculpted landscape that responded to site conditions.[16]

At Dulles, Kiley designed a landscape that provided a frame and counterweight for the iconic terminal building and its hippodrome-shaped parking area, featuring gridded mass plantings of a variety of tree and shrub species and evergreen groundcover. Azaleas, firethorn, and abelias provided bright color throughout the seasons, and through the use of evergreen groundcover, the airport could always appear neatly set in the larger landscape. Eastern red cedar planted in grids along the approach roads and at the corners concealed service buildings and formed a permanent dark evergreen frame and a link to the mixed forests and woods beyond the airport boundary. The tree plantings on the medians of the access road and the dogwoods along its outer slopes (which were never realized) were intended to "compress space" for approaching car drivers and to channel views, highlighting the effect of the terminal building and its control tower. Kiley intended the gridded tree plantings to provide for both easy maintenance and visual interest, especially when viewed from a moving car.[17]

In contrast, it was the aerial view from departing and landing planes that inspired his idea for "horizontal mural[s] beyond human scale" consisting of a checkerboard pattern of red and white flowering azaleas beneath the rectangular blocks of trees that framed the terminal area.[18] Although this checkerboard planting was not carried out, an explosion of color to greet travelers was realized through the planting of rows of red azalea flanking the terminal building

and of firethorn underplanted with creeping myrtle on the gently sloping edges of the parking lot. The vegetation's color brought attention to the terminal area, and the plants' low height ensured the prominence of the architecture.

Kiley's planting plan turned the parking lot into a monumental entrance court to the terminal. Besides the jet, the car was celebrated in the airport's overall design, and the terminal became a transfer station between automobile and air traffic. The transition from the immediate terminal landscape, with its geometrical planting beds in which plants are positioned with engineered precision, to Virginia's countryside—today engulfed by suburban sprawl—was established through loose forest plantings along the approach roads and the design of an eight-hectare lake as retention basin for water runoff from the terminal building.[19] Kiley worked within the green belt of trees (some original, some newly planted) that surrounded the airport grounds to provide a screen and noise buffer.[20] The FAA planned a reforestation program to assure a solid 300-meter-deep timber belt along the airport perimeter that would be extended to 760 meters at the ends of runways.[21]

Other airports also sought the expertise of landscape designers, in particular airports that realized their potential in the tourist industry. When a new terminal building at Honolulu International Airport was built in the early 1960s, a fountain made from local lava rock and illuminated at night with colored lights was positioned along the approach road to welcome visitors. Landscape architect Richard C. Tongg complemented the new terminal building with the so-called cultural gardens. Enclosed by the

16   For I. M. Pei & Associates' work on the tower, see Philip Jodidio, ed., *I. M. Pei: Complete Works* (New York: Rizzoli, 2008), 92–95; "New Tower to Grace Airports," *Architectural Forum* (November 1963): 113–114; Walter McQuade, "A Better View at Airports," *Fortune* (February 1967): 1959–60.

17   See "Landscape Report for Dulles International Airport, prepared by Office of Dan Kiley, Site and Landscape Consultant, March 10, 1960"; Sonja Dümpelmann, *Flights of Imagination: Aviation, Landscape, Design* (Charlottesville, VA: University of Virginia Press, 2014), 62–65.

18   Dan Kiley and Jane Amidon, *Dan Kiley in His Own Words* (London: Thames and Hudson, 1999), 41.

19   See Federal Aviation Agency, *Dulles*.

20   See Ibid.

21   Ibid., 23.

View of the Japanese Garden, part of the cultural gardens designed by Richard C. Tongg at Honolulu International Airport, March 1964.

terminal on a triangular piece of ground and divided into three parts, the cultural gardens included a Chinese Garden, a Japanese Garden, and a Hawaiian Garden, reflecting the cultures that had most shaped island life. The gardens were an expression of ideas that Tongg and Loraine E. Kuck had explored in their 1939 book, *The Tropical Garden*. In the tropics, they noted, cultures mingled, and therefore "[design] details from one source do not appear too strange in the other."[22] At the airport, the cultural gardens were intended to introduce visitors to the islands' culture and nature, notwithstanding the widespread repression of native Hawaiian customs and culture at the time and US-Japanese tensions that followed the Japanese attack on Pearl Harbor. Like Dulles, Honolulu's international airport was considered a model for a successful airport landscape.

"AIRPORT BEAUTIFICATION" AND "HUSH PARKS"

In the mid-1960s, the airport attracted the attention of "Lady Bird" Johnson, who after her husband's election as President in 1964 made the nation's beautification her mission. The First Lady wanted to make sure that beauty and culture would not be neglected in the pursuit of national economic growth. Lyndon Johnson addressed Congress on February 8, 1965, with the mandate to "introduce into all our planning, our programs, our building, and our growth a conscious and active concern for the values of beauty."[23] Some months later, the 1965 White House Conference on Natural Beauty brought together conservationists, industrialists, government officials, and private citizens to discuss solutions to many environmental problems such as suburbanization, the underground installation

22 Loraine E. Kuck and Richard C. Tongg, *The Tropical Garden* (New York: MacMillan Company, 1939), 54.

23 Federal Aviation Administration, *America's Airport Beautification Awards Program* (Washington, DC: Government Printing Office, 1967).

of utilities, automobile junkyards, and highway design. The conference provided a platform for ideas that would also influence the treatment of the airport landscape. Inspired by the successful comprehensive design of Dulles International Airport, the federal government initiated an Airport Beautification Awards Program in 1967.[24]

To participate in the awards program, airport authorities were asked to submit "landscape projects that screened trash collection points, aircraft parts, equipment storage places, and other unsightly areas; and that planted shrubbery, trees, and groundcover that not only beautified the premises but also took into account bird hazards, local soil conditions and climate, and plants that attracted parasitic animals; the selection of trees and shrubbery to help reduce aircraft noise." Projects that improved the appearance of public areas, parking lots, access roads, and other zones that were immediately visible to airport visitors also qualified. Restoration of old airport buildings and the elimination of dangerous aerial wires threatening helicopters and airplanes were also of interest. Furthermore, the construction of special aviation exhibit halls, community-wide airport "clean-up" campaigns, and programs designed to stimulate further community participation in airport beautification efforts had a chance of obtaining an award. As a brochure announced, the program was to provide an incentive for long-range beauty development programs and immediate, low-cost "face-lifting" activities that would position airports as keystones of civic pride and hospitality, and "vibrant examples of aesthetic and cultural life."[25] Airport authorities were encouraged to integrate their initiatives into their communities' comprehensive land use plans.[26] By the end of the 1960s, it had

become clear that every airport needed an "*airport area plan* which integrate[d] the airport into the urban complex."[27]

In June 1967, Mrs. Johnson presented the first award for airport beautification to Mayor Milton Graham of Phoenix for the city's Sky Harbor Airport, which only a year before had begun a $2.5-million expansion program. The citation was given for "offering an example of how a metropolitan airport can be made an integral part of a city's aesthetic, cultural and economic life."[28] The First Lady's airport beautification campaign was not without precedent. In the 1930s, designers and critics had argued for the airports' ordered development and comprehensive design. Under the influence of the City Beautiful movement, many advocated for an "airport beautiful," and utopian airport designs in the 1920s and 1930s often reflected a Beaux-Arts influence. Airports were conceived of as small cities, with hangars symmetrically flanking the main terminal building and an axial central approach road often embedded in picturesque parkland that would also include recreational facilities such as swimming pools.

The association of airports and parks seemed logical given that early flight was considered both a scientific and a recreational pursuit, requiring extensive open space. Many plans were made to locate airports within parks and urban park systems, and in some cities the parks department administered the airport in the early years. In the 1920s and 1930s, landscape architects began to investigate airports and aviation as thesis projects; to design airport landscapes; and to incorporate the airport as a subject into their manuals and books. Airport planners and officials believed that landscape architects'

24   For the First Lady's visit to National Airport, see Lewis L. Gould, *Lady Bird Johnson and the Environment* (Lawrence, KS: University Press of Kansas, 1988), 82. As a consequence of her visit, "Lady Bird" Johnson advised the administrator of the Federal Aviation Agency that the appearance of these areas could be improved through the planting of shrubs and flowers.

25   Federal Aviation Administration, *Airport Beautification.*

26   Ibid.

27   Conway, Jr., "Crisis."

28   James H. Winchester, "Sweet Smell of Success: Phoenix Is Deodorizing Its Stockyards and ...," *New York Times*, Dec 11, 1966, 501; Also see *Los Angeles Times*, June 7, 1967, 2.

contributions to "airport beautification"[29] not only pleased the eye but, due to their psychological effects, could also prevent crashes.[30]

Both the construction and the improvement and beautification of airports came to be part of the Works Progress Administration (WPA) airports and airways program in the 1930s. The program sought to provide work opportunities during the Depression while benefiting national transportation and security, and fostering rural development. For example, a system of small airports—"air parks"—was planned for construction in Alabama. Air parks combined runways with golf courses, tennis courts, swimming pools, and other recreational facilities. As one promotional brochure announced, an air park was both a part of the nation's airport network and "a park and a beauty spot to be enjoyed by everyone."[31] By combining aviation and recreation, and by turning small airports into a new type of park, municipal park departments became responsible for transportation infrastructure, ostensibly relieving the financial strain that the maintenance of airports placed on small communities. "Maintenance of the field becomes simply a matter of maintenance of the park," the WPA creatively argued.[32] Within the WPA's airports and airways program, workers were employed to grade and clear land; lay out concrete runways; install lighting and radio communication systems; paint airway markers; build terminals, hangars, swimming pools, and other recreational facilities; and lay out lawns and plantings surrounding the airport facilities.[33]

Many of the WPA projects in the 1930s were not dissimilar to the projects promoted through the Airport Beautification Awards Program in the 1960s. One of the most common arguments against the later campaigns, however, was their social and functional inadequacy. As the term "beautification"—which the First Lady herself disliked—implied, the initiatives ran the risk of being understood as merely cosmetic efforts. This had been the foremost criticism of the City Beautiful movement by male designers and planners for whom "beautification" implied the early 20th-century female-led city cleanup campaigns.[34] To John Brinckerhoff Jackson, the presidential campaign was nothing else. For the advocate of the American vernacular landscape, the First Lady's initiative did not propose "a permanent alteration in the environment but a disguising of the ugliness, like a gangster's coffin, under a mass of greenery and flowers." Jackson posed that "beautification of this sort lasts for a month or two, or however long it says on the package of seeds." For him the campaign—"a Garden Club solution" and "hopelessly superficial"—lacked stability. For a real change of attitude among the American public, Jackson argued, policy changes would have to be made to counter the public attitude that "whatever is old is obsolete, and whatever is obsolete is discarded."[35]

Although Lady Bird Johnson was caught in the gendered stereotypes of her campaign that included the use of "beautification" in the name, she did seek to influence policy decisions and the development of the nation's rural and urban landscape.[36] The Airport Beautification Awards Program aimed to reevaluate the nation's

29   Karl Baptiste Lohmann, *Landscape Architecture in the Modern World* (Champaign, IL: Garrard Press, 1941), 130.

30   See, for example, the chapter on "The Design of Airports" in Lohmann's *Landscape Architecture*; and the chapter "Airport Development" in Richard Sudell's *Landscape Gardening* (London and Melbourne: Ward, Lock, 1933), 417–418. At Harvard University, landscape architect Henry Vincent Hubbard carried out an airport study with colleagues in city planning; one of his students, Howard K. Menhinick, graduated with a thesis on municipal

airports in landscape architecture in city planning in 1926. For more on landscape architects' role and involvement in airport planning and design, see Dümpelmann, *Flights of Imagination*, chapters 1, 2, and 6.

31   "America Spreads Its Wings." Brochure issued by the WPA. Washington, DC: US Government Printing Office, 1937.

32   Ibid.

33   Ibid.

34   Lewis L. Gould, *Lady Bird Johnson and the Environment* (Lawrence, KS: University of Kansas Press, 1988), 60.

35   John Brinckerhoff Jackson, "The Message on Natural Beauty," *Landscape* 14, no. 3 (1965): 1.

36   For an elaborate assessment of Lady Bird Johnson's role in the campaign see Gould, *Lady Bird Johnson*, in particular pages 51–75.

Plan and bird's-eye view of model air park projected for small towns in Alabama.

Blueprints showing diagrams of a prototypical X-, T-, and L-plan for landing fields at Alabama air parks that combine runways with golf courses, athletic fields, and playgrounds.

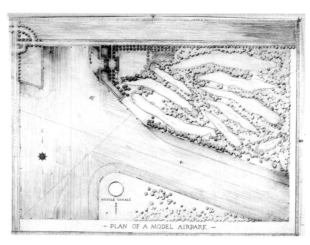

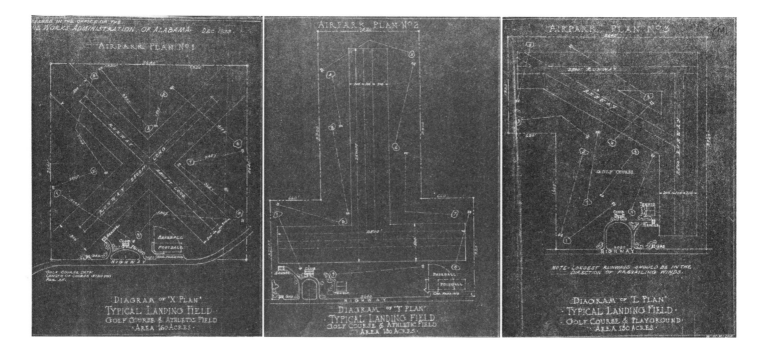

seemingly obsolete airports, although landscape design was indeed mostly used to camouflage unsightly areas. What the awards program did achieve was to publicly recognize the airport as a designed landscape, an integral component of the designed environment. It countered the common perception of the airport as a purely technological infrastructure that had by the 1960s become a meaningless wasteland. Instead it framed the airport as a place, albeit one characterized by fleetingness, movement, and transition.

Despite the move to address airport landscapes, a 1972 report for the US Department of Transportation stated that the "undefined amorphous open areas" of airports and the "unimpressive" connections between airports and cities, as well as the haphazard development in the airports' vicinity, needed attention. It pointed out that the airport's visual impact on nearby communities could not be separated from the impact of aircraft noise and airport-related traffic.[37]

A first attempt to address this issue were "hush parks"—tree plantings around airports designed to absorb and break up sound waves. Coined by Najeeb E. Halaby, FAA administrator (1961–1965) at the 1965 White House Conference, "hush parks" were considered a means to reduce noise contamination in residential areas near airports.[38] Only a few decades earlier, landscape architects had become alert to the problem of noise and the role they could play in its abatement through designing for sound deflection,

reflection, and absorption. In one of the first publications to mention this work, landscape architect Ralph Rodney Root elaborated on the breaking up of sound waves by tree plantings, especially in the case of airports and sites for motorized vehicles such as entrance drives, motor courts, and public highways.[39] By the 1960s, experiments had been carried out determining the propagation of sound from jet engines and the noise-reducing capacity of different tree species and their depth of planting. A decade later, studies were undertaken specifically about how to screen off aircraft noise with the help of forests. But it was clear that much research in this area still needed to be done, especially because sound proofing against motor traffic was different from countering aircraft noise.[40]

A "BATTLE AGAINST NATURE"?

Since the 1920s, airports have stood at the intersection of nature and technology. They have been a site for the negotiation of environmental and ecological concerns. In the 1940s, British aeronautical engineer Sydney E. Veale had argued that "modern airports must be manmade," and that nature had to be "rectified" in the process by scarring "the surface with broad, straight deep-laid runways," felling trees, excavating and leveling, and blasting and drilling to make a site.[41] By then, airports had evolved from

37   CLM/Systems Inc., "Airports and Their Environment: A Guide to Environmental Planning," prepared for the US Department of Transportation (September 1972), 183–184.

38   See White House Conference on Natural Beauty, Washington, DC, 1965: Beauty for America, Proceedings, May 24–25, 1965. (Washington, DC: Government Printing Office, 1965), 85; "New Tower."

39   See Ralph Rodney Root, Contourscaping (Chicago: Ralph Fletcher Seymour, 1941), 230–235. The need for noise reduction in aircraft had been realized by this time as well, and first studies to this effect were carried out during World War II at Harvard University with the

objective of quieting the interiors of long-range bombers. See Leo L. Beranek and H. Wayne Rudmose, "Sound Control in Airplanes," Journal of the Acoustical Society of America 19, no. 2 (March 1947): 357–364; S.S. Stevens, J.P. Egan, T.H. Waterman, J. Miller, R.H. Knapp, and S.C. Rome, "Effects of Noise on Psychomotor Efficiency and Noise Reduction in Aircraft as Related to Communication Annoyance and Aural Injury," OSRK Report no. 274 (December 1, 1941).

40   See G.B.V. Wendorff, "Schützt der Wald vor Fluglärm? Gedanken zum forstlichen Lärmschutz," Forstarchiv 45, no. 1 (1974): 6–11; T.F.W. Embleton, "Sound Propagation in Homogeneous Deciduous and Evergreen Woods," The Journal of the Acoustical Society

of America 35 (1963): 1119–1125. In Germany, the Institute of Landscape Construction and Garden Art at the Technical University Berlin led by landscape architect and professor Hermann Mattern conducted the first scientific study in the field on plants as material to stifle traffic noise between 1962 and 1965. Also see Franz J. Meister, "Geräuschmessungen an Verkehrsflugzeugen und ihre hörpsychologische Bewertung," Arbeitsgemeinschaft für Forschung des Landes Nordrhein-Westfalen 94 (Cologne and Opladen: Westdeutscher Verlag, 1961), 141–171.

41   Sydney E. Veale, To-morrow's Airliners, Airways, and Airports (London: Pilot Press Ltd., 1945), 247.

an "almost pastoral phase" characterized by sheep grazing on airfields to a site design determined by engine power, newly developed materials, and transportation and transfer logistics.[42] However, by the 1960s it had become clear that despite technological progress, nature could not be controlled entirely, and it was not only the weather that could create havoc. Wildlife, mostly birds and mammals, but also reptiles such as the diamondback terrapin that in 2014 led to flight delays at John F. Kennedy International Airport, were among the most difficult things to manage.[43] Then as now, airports are often among the few expansive open spaces left in our increasingly urbanizing territories. As scientists have shown, airports fulfill important ecological functions and are attractive foraging and nesting habitats for many wildlife species, in particular raptors and other birds.[44] Besides causing air, noise, soil, and water pollution, it is the airport's function as habitat and its position within larger ecological systems that have caused controversy and conflict.

In October 1960, an accident occurred at Boston Logan International Airport that drew national attention to this conflict. Shortly after takeoff, a four-engine Lockheed Electra turbo-prop heading to Philadelphia hit a flock of starlings and plunged into Winthrop Bay, killing 62 of the 72 people on board. The accident reinforced what some newspapers called "a battle against nature."[45] While bird-control measures, such as shotgun patrols to scare nesting gulls, were already in place at the time of the accident, and clam digging along the shore was prohibited as a consequence of the crash, the deadly event triggered further experiments and a national discussion about wildlife management and "bird strike" hazard at airports.

Bird-control methods considered at Logan included distribution of strychnine-laced bread, electrocution, and spraying eggs to render them sterile.[46] The airport was spending around $60,000 a year to repel birds and improve safety, yet the futility of all methods was clear. As Ephraim A. Brest, chairman of the Massachusetts Port Authority, noted in early 1961, birds could not be controlled or eliminated from the airport and its surroundings. He therefore implored aeronautical engineers to design aircraft engines that scared birds or "shielded them from air intakes, or pulverized and burned [them] in some manner so that little or no damage will result."[47] If nature could not be controlled and managed to create an environment that was secure for flight, technology appeared as the last resort. Yet in addition to research into jet engines that were more resistant to "foreign matter ingestion," the FAA entered into a research contract with the Department of the Interior's Bureau of Fisheries and Wildlife to investigate potential biological control of birds at airports,

42   Banham, "Obsolescent Airport," 252.

43   For the diamondback terrapins, see Nate Schweber, "Studying What Lures Turtles to a Tarmac at Kennedy Airport," New York Times, July 4, 2014, A14.

44   See, for example, Bradley F. Blackwell, Travis L. DeVault, Esteban Fernández-Juricic, and Richard A. Dolbeer, "Wildlife Collisions with Aircraft: A Missing Component of Land-Use Planning for Airports," Landscape and Urban Planning 93 (2009): 1–9. The Boston accident was an important event in the more recent history of jet aircraft in the United States. However, birds and flying machines have had earlier collisions. In 1905, one of Orville and Wilbur Wright's early test flights in Dayton killed a bird. In turn, the first recorded human death resulting from a collision between bird and flying machine has been reported as occurring in April 1912 in Long Beach, California. There, Cal Rogers struck a gull that jammed the flight controls of his linen-covered biplane, causing it to crash into the ocean. For these early collisions, see Wilbur Wright's diary entry for September 7, 1905, Wilbur and Orville Wright Papers at the Library of Congress; H. Blokpoel, Bird Hazards to Aircraft (Ottawa: Clarke, Irwin & Co. Ltd., 1976); Tom Kelly and John Allan, "Ecological Effects of Aviation," in The Ecology of Transportation: Managing Mobility for the Environment, ed. John Davenport and Julia L. Davenport (Dordrecht: Springer, 2006), 5–24.

45   John F. Halloran, Executive Director of the Massachusetts Port Authority, in a letter to Najeeb Haleby, Administrator of the Federal Aviation Agency, on July 7, 1961. Folder 3, Box 53, Records of the Federal Aviation Administration, RG 237, National Archives and Records Administration. For the Boston Electra crash, see Michael N. Kalafatas, Bird Strike: The Crash of the Boston Electra (Waltham, MA: Brandeis University Press, 2010).

46   Address of Chairman Ephraim A. Brest from the Massachusetts Port Authority before the General Electric Aircraft Accessory Turbine Management Association, Logan International Airport, Wednesday Evening, April 26, 1961. Folder 3, Box 53, Records of the Federal Aviation Administration, RG 237, National Archives and Records Administration.

47   Ibid.

48   See documents in Folder 3, Box 53, Records of the Federal Aviation Administration, RG 237, National Archives and Records Administration. This method had already been used at European airports for decades. At Berlin-Gatow (see pages 126–127), an airport used by the RAF in the Cold War, the British military used falcons in 1948 and 1949 during the Berlin Blockade to keep the airfield free from swarms of birds. See "Jagdfalken für Gatow," Der Tagesspiegel, October 22, 1948.

Ornithologist Roxie Collie S. Laybourne (1912–2003) worked in the Division of Birds at the United States National Museum and with the Bird and Mammal Laboratories, Fish and Wildlife Service. She was involved in identifying the birds that collided with the Lockheed Electra turboprop at Boston Logan airport in October 1960. In the 1960s, she created the field of forensic ornithology, studying minute fragments of bird feathers to identify which birds were ingested into aircraft engines, often causing crashes.

including the use of trained falcons.[48] The final 1968 report, however, concentrated its recommendations on landscape and habitat management.

Proposed measures included filling water bodies; eliminating food sources such as sewer outfalls, refuse heaps, and fish piers; keeping grass at a certain height to deter birds from nesting and foraging; and dredging mudflats, sand, and gravel bars below tide level.[49] Yet by 1968, few of these measures had been carried out at Logan. Marshes and freshwater ponds had not been filled, and the mudflats surrounding the airport had not been dredged. Although progress had been made in the establishment of a new sewage-treatment plant on Deer Island, fish were still being dumped into the harbor at Boston's Fish Pier, providing an ample food source for herring gulls.[50]

In contrast to airport authorities in other countries, particularly in Europe, that make extensive use of falcons and other biological wildlife management efforts, the FAA has been reluctant to adopt or maintain many of these methods at airports in the United States. The exclusive use of "softer" biological methods has not convinced FAA officials, and at many airports lethal methods (including shooting birds) have become the rule. Sharpshooters employed at John F. Kennedy International Airport killed 52,235 gulls between 1991 and 1997.[51] In 1996 the airport's wildlife biologist began deploying falcons—that, if improperly trained, pose a strike risk themselves—but in 2011 the airport ceased the practice. In 2014, controversy surrounded the airport killing of three snowy owls that, animal rights activists argued, could easily have been caught and taken to a different location, as is current practice at Logan International Airport.[52]

Increasing attention to environmental concerns as well as economic and political pressures have led airport authorities to consider their land suitable for other uses, such as animal pasturage and beekeeping, to foster an image of an environmentally sensitive and responsible aviation industry. Contemporary economic reasons for this "green" aviation politics notwithstanding, today's hybrid use of the airport recalls its origins. When Wilbur and Orville Wright transferred their aerial experiments from Kitty Hawk, North Carolina, to Dayton, Ohio, in 1904, they flew out of a cow pasture; the cows had to be penned in at the southern end of the field during flights. When the first airports were built, sheep were used to keep the airfield's grass short and the ground compacted.

In contrast, once the airport had become a completely manufactured site dominated by technology, designers tended to regard its natural elements as obstacles. Landscape architecture professor Florence B. Robinson argued in 1948 that noise was a problem for the engineers to deal with, while the "ugliness, barrenness, glare, and dust are overcome largely by proper planting" and were therefore in the landscape architect's domain. Robinson demanded that cities and airports be developed together and that airport officials "maintain the port and its immediate surroundings in a pleasing and agreeable state" through proper planting and landscape design.[53] In Robinson's eyes, airport planting was to give expression to the airport's position and function as hinge between "the infinity of space and terrestrial solidity," offering pleasurable

49   See John L. Seubert, "Control of Birds On and Around Airports," October 1968, US Department of the Interior, Bureau of Sport Fisheries and Wildlife, Division of Wildlife Research. Washington, DC, 1968, 8–10.

50   See ibid., 10–11.

51   Kalafatas, Bird Strike, 114.

52   See Barry Newman, "Falcons at New York's JFK Airport Join the Flock of the Unemployed," Wall Street Journal, April 29, 2011; Charlie LeDuff, "Birds on Your Runway? Scare Them Off with Tougher Birds," New York Times, Nov. 17, 1996, CY12; Stephanie Clifford, "Suit Says Owl Killings at Kennedy Airport Were Excessive," New York Times, August 1, 2014. For the use of falcons at European airports, see, for example, Stefan Ulrich, "Die Himmelfeger," Süddeutsche Zeitung, May 17, 2010;

Miriam Opresnik, "Falken für die Flugsicherung," Hamburger Abendblatt, December 28, 2004.

53   Florence B. Robinson, "Landscape Planting for Airports," Aeronatics Bulletin no. 2 (University of Illinois, 1948), 6.

scenery seen from the air and on the ground. Representative of landscape architecture's professional orientation at the time, her argument was based solely on the aesthetics of landscape design and planting. Even if it was clear then (as now) that plantings should not obstruct sightlines and flight paths, their role in wildlife management was not yet discussed. Only since the 1990s has sustained attention been paid to plantings' environmental functions. When West 8 consulted on the landscape at Amsterdam Airport Schiphol in the 1990s, birch trees were chosen to afforest the surroundings, lining bike paths, parking lots, and roads. Not only are birch trees a pioneer species in this region of the Netherlands, but the tree does not attract birds.

The designers proposed the planting of clover and the keeping of bees on airport areas that are free from construction. Beekeeping has since become a popular environmental initiative at airports, both for the production of honey that is now often sold at the airports and as a biomarker to detect pollutants. Hamburg airport began beekeeping in 1999, followed by the airports in Düsseldorf, Frankfurt, Dresden, Hannover, Leipzig/Halle, Nuremberg, Munich, and finally Copenhagen, Malmø, Lambert-St. Louis International, Chicago's O'Hare, and Seattle-Tacoma International (SeaTac).[54] The latter two are among a handful of airports in the United States that are currently also experimenting with animal pasturage as a wildlife management measure on their grounds, as illustrated in this volume (see pages 38 and 39). By introducing goats, llamas, and burros that scare away coyotes and deer, the airport authorities at O'Hare and SeaTac are promoting their "green" image and introducing a more sustainable maintenance method on grounds that are hard to access with mechanical equipment.[55]

A JETPORT IN THE EVERGLADES

The high potential for "bird strikes" (or "bird-plane strikes," as it was perhaps more accurately phrased in one of the first studies on the subject) was among the reasons that the Everglades Jetport in South Florida—a project touted as the world's first new jetport for the supersonic age, which had broken ground in 1968—was not carried out as planned.[56] The controversial proposal was one of the first infrastructure projects subject to environmental impact assessments even before federal legislation had been passed. The discussion around the Everglades Jetport that culminated in 1969–1970 not only set the stage for environmental legislation but also provided President Richard Nixon with a programmatic and promotional opportunity to usher in the 1970s as the environmental decade.

The planned jetport site was in the Big Cypress Swamp, a prime feeding ground for Florida's wading birds. The airport had been designed for a 39-square-mile area (1½ times the area of Manhattan) that surpassed even Dulles, Idlewild, and Dallas/Fort Worth in size. It was to turn the Miami region, an area witnessing unprecedented urban development due to the introduction of air conditioning, the application of pesticides, and new earth-moving technology, into a new aviation center. Its planners

54   Danielle Beurteaux, "Bees Are Now Cleared for Landing at Airports," *New York Times*, February 19, 2015.

55   See Monica Guzman, "Sea-Tac Airport Get Goats to Do the Weeding," *Seattle PI*, September 9, 2008. http://blog.seattlepi.com/thebigblog/2008/09/09/sea-tac-airport-gets-goats-to-do-the-weeding/; Jason Kayser, "Baa! O'Hare Turns to Goats to Clear Airfield Brush," *Associated Press*, August 13, 2013. http://bigstory.ap.org/article/baa-ohare-turns-goats-clear-airfield-brush.

56   See US Department of the Interior, "Environmental Impact of the Big Cypress Swamp Jetport" (September 1969); B. F. McPherson, C. Y. Hendrix, Howard Klein, and H. M. Tyus, "The Environment of South Florida: A Summary Report," Geological Survey Professional Paper 1011 (US Department of the Interior, Washington, DC: United States Government Printing Office, 1976); Philip Wylie, "Confrontation in the Everglades: Against All Odds, the Birds Have Won," *New York Times*, February 1, 1970, XX1. On the Everglades Jetport project, see

Michael Grunwald, *The Swamp: The Everglades, Florida, and the Politics of Paradise* (New York: Simon and Schuster, 2006), 254–263.

contended that the new airport would be the nucleus of a larger multimodal transportation corridor that would attract urban development and extend from Miami on the Atlantic Ocean to Naples on the Gulf of Mexico.[57] However, what planners in 1968 were still promoting as the advantages of the new jetport site—reduced noise pollution above cities and redirected air traffic to uninhabited zones—turned out to be its greatest disadvantage. While airport promoters argued that the swampy site was ideal because of its remoteness and that the Everglades would ultimately protect against uncontrolled urban growth, environmentalists illustrated that the entire ecosystem would suffer through air, soil, water, and noise pollution.

By 1969, negative public sentiment surrounding the jetport had grown, and the project had become a symbol for environmental opposition nationally. Would "man . . . turn a refuge into wasteland" through the construction of the jetport, asked one *New York Times* article.[58] Environmentalists, including members of the Audubon Society, Friends of the Earth, and Friends of the Everglades, an organization founded by the feminist Marjory Stoneman Douglas, Florida's Rachel Carson, condemned the plans.[59] Their stance was bolstered by research led by Department of the Interior scientist Luna Leopold, son of the influential American environmentalist Aldo Leopold. The hydrologist was very clear: a commercial airport would destroy the unique ecosystem of the

Everglades, which had been made a national park in 1934. Whereas most public concerns focused on environmental degradation, the Leopold report also drew attention to the social threats of the plan. Air and noise pollution would affect the indigenous Miccosukee inhabitants of the area, and developmental pressures caused by the jetport would destabilize their social and economic lives.[60]

Yet a report by the National Academy of Sciences supported the jetport's construction and considered its move north of the Everglades an option to avoid further conflict.[61] In a strategic move to push the project through, the Dade County Commissioners hired environmentalist and former Secretary of the Interior Stewart L. Udall and his environmental planning consulting firm, the Overview Group, to prepare a plan that would minimize adverse affects of the jetport on the national park.[62] The firm's proposal, hailed as one of the first to seriously address the environmental consequences of a major development project, was an airport without terminal buildings that would be accessible to passengers via futuristic high-speed rail or air-cushion vehicles.[63]

When President Nixon halted the project in January 1970 and agreed to federal support for land acquisition at an alternative site, one runway had already been built for aviation training. Training flights and the search for an alternative airport site continued through the 1970s. By then, however, environmentalists had also gained ground through new legislative measures, and

57   See Earl M. Starnes, "Airport Operation and Urban Planning," in *Master Planning of Air Space: A Total Systems Approach*, 66–86.

58   Brooks Atkinson, "The Everglades: Will Man Turn a Refuge into Wasteland?" *New York Times*, January 11, 1969, 35.

59   For conservationist and feminist Marjory Stoneman Douglas and her role in the protection of the Everglades against the planned jetport, see Grunwald, *The Swamp*, 257–258; Jack E. Davis, "Up from the Sawgrass: Marjory Stoneman Douglas and the Influence of Female Activism in Florida Conservation," in *Making Waves: Female Activists in Twentieth-Century Florida*, ed. Jack E. Davis and Raymond Arsenault (Gainesville, FL: University Press of Florida, 2003), 147–176; Jack E. Davis, "Green

Awakening: Social Activism and the Evolution of Marjory Stoneman Douglas's Environmental Consciousness," *The Florida Historical Quarterly* 80, no. 1 (July 2001), 43–77; *Mary Joy Breton, Women Pioneers for the Environment* (Boston: Northeastern University Press, 1998), 237–245; Marjory Stoneman Douglas, *Voice of the River: An Autobiography* (with John Rothchild; Englewood, FL: Pineapple Press, 1987), 224–226.

60   US Department of the Interior, "Environmental Impact," 7, 9.

61   See "Sciences Academy Supports Jetport Near Everglades," *New York Times*, September 19, 1969, 93; James Malone, "Jetport Studied to Death?" *Miami Herald*, September 7, 1969, 1B, 8B.

62   Homer Bigart, "Naturalists Shudder as Officials Hail Everglades Jetport," *New York Times*, Aug. 11, 1969, 37. Udall's position in the commission appears ambiguous, although in a conversation with the Under Secretary of the Department of the Interior he pointed out that he had made it clear to the Dade County Port Authority that he "would not bring his firm in 'as window dressing', but only if they were willing to take a hard look at alternatives." See memorandum of the Under Secretary to the Secretary of the Department of the Interior, July 1, 1969. Walter J. Hickel papers, Archives and Special Collections, Consortium Library, University of Alaska Anchorage, Box 5, Folder 7.

63   Bayard Webster, "New Type of Jetport Urged for Miami," *New York Times*, September 28, 1969, 82.

the jetport was not built. On January 1, President Nixon signed the Environmental Protection Act into law, requiring developers of any federally authorized project to submit an environmental impact statement. The 1970 Airport and Airway Development Act incorporated parts of this legislation, forcing airport developers to hold public hearings to explore the environmental impact of their projects and to safeguard natural resources and protect environmental quality. It enabled the Department of Transportation, in consultation with other agencies, to block any project whose impact would be adverse, unless no reasonable alternative existed and all possible steps had been taken to minimize harmful effects.[64] In 1971 the FAA declared that the "environmental issue...may well be the greatest challenge to aviation in the '70s."[65]

LANDSCAPES OF OPPOSITION

From Atlanta to Minneapolis-St. Paul and St. Louis, and from New York and Boston to Portland and San Jose, people were opposing jetport projects and airport expansions.[66] The movement in the United States arose from the increasing obsolescence of airports built before the Jet Age, growing environmentalist sentiment, and suburbanization with its accompanying NIMBY ("not in my backyard") attitude, but the overall phenomenon was international. Airports have always confronted larger societal issues, which now often reflect the tension between global and local economies and desires.

In the 1970s, airports became the flashpoint for debates about environmental degradation and pollution, land grabs, and economic growth—a "symbolic landscape of opposition."[67]

Narita airport in Japan and Frankfurt airport in Germany spawned the two most well-known anti-airport movements, which formed landscapes of opposition in the 1960s and have led to resurging, and sometimes violent, protests ever since. For the farmers at Narita, the expropriation and transformation of their land—once part of an Imperial estate with a famous grove of cherry trees—into a new international airport signified a despoliation of land and a betrayal of culture and tradition. As Lisa Peattie has pointed out, the destruction of the cherry trees, symbolic of the values of traditional Japanese life, caused some farmers to threaten ceremonial mass suicide.[68] Student activists protested capitalist development and the eventual use of the airport by the United States military. Captured with much empathy in Shinsuke Ogawa's documentary films *Summer in Narita* (1967) and *Narita: The Peasants of the Second Fortress* (1968), militant and peaceful protesters alike built a fortified village that included towers and underground bunkers. As David E. Apter has argued, these structures "represent a moral architecture...a superior moral existence based on nurture and cultivation in contrast to the careless ruthlessness of the runways and buildings of an airport and the industrialization, pollution, ecological disaster they represented."[69]

In Frankfurt as well, a "village of huts" (*Hüttendorf*) was built as a "village of resistance"

64   See Committee on Public Works and Transportation, US House of Representatives, *Airport and Airway Development Act of 1970* (Washington, DC: US Government Printing Office, 1976), Part II, Section 12 (c), and (f) on page 5.

65   Federal Aviation Administration, *National Aviation System Plan: 1972–1981* (Washington, DC: US Department of Transportation, Federal Aviation Administration, March 1971), 23.

66   See, for example, Robert Lindsey, "New Jetports Held Up By Protest Movements," *New York Times*, July 11, 1971, 1.

67   For airport opposition movements, see Suleiman Osman's talk, "The Anti-Airport Landscape: Local Protest Against Airports in the 1960s and 1970s," Airport Landscape conference, November 14–15, 2013, Harvard University Graduate School of Design. For a first elaboration on the topic, see Lisa R. Peattie, *Planners and Protesters: Airport Opposition as Social Movement* Institute for Urban Studies Monograph Series, no. 9 (College Park, MD: University of Maryland, 1991).

68   Peattie, *Planners and Protesters*, 11.

69   David E. Apter, *Rethinking Development: Modernization, Dependency, and Postmodern Politics* (Newbury Park, CA: Sage Publications, 1987), 242–243. For Ogawa's Sanrizuka Series, see Abé Mark Nornes, *Forest of Pressure: Ogawa Shinsuke and Postwar Japanese Documentary* (Minneapolis: University of Minnesota Press, 2007).

in the woods adjacent to the site of a new four-kilometer-long west runway planned for the expansion of commercial air traffic at an airport that in the 1970s was still shared with the American military.[70] Following similar protest movements against nuclear power stations and reprocessing plants and in defense of urban squatting, many citizen initiatives and local action groups rallied against the airport development. They ranged from groups that opposed the expected increase in noise pollution to activists who congregated around issues of land use, environmental destruction, and capitalist development. By building a vernacular village in the woods, the protesters gave form to what many in a somewhat romantic and nostalgic spirit associated with the establishment of an alternative community and a new social utopia.[71]

These rustic alternative landscapes of opposition contrasted starkly with the modern sleek terminal buildings designed to facilitate fast movement. In an interesting twist of history, the informal wood constructions built by the protesters resembled the rough-hewn aesthetic of the huts that the WPA had promoted for construction at air parks within its airports and airways program in the 1930s. Despite their different genesis, objectives, places, and times, both movements sought to root themselves in their localities and vernacular traditions. They made use of local materials and the local work force, and in the case of the WPA in the 1930s, quite consciously wedded a modern infrastructure to designed parkland that was already anchored in the community.

The symbolism of nature as a local force to combat global capital loomed large in the 1960s'

and 1970s' protest movements against airports elsewhere as well. At a small airport near Sisteron in the French rural municipality of Vaumeilh in Haute Provence, protesters marched on the airport singing a revolutionary song in regional dialect, covered the tarmac with dirt, and planted thyme, considered a symbolic and traditional plant of the Languedoc, where it grows profusely. Covering the airport with the local cultural landscape was to protect it against future charter jet planes.[72] More than elsewhere perhaps, in the United States concerns about environmental justice further incited airport debates. As a reaction to Boston's airport expansion plans in the 1960s, citizens protested aircraft noise that affected the working-class neighborhood adjacent to the airport and the anticipated destruction of Wood Island Park designed by F. L. Olmsted.[73] What planners considered a rundown plot of land, residents valued as a shady haven and a "traditional place to gather and play."[74]

NEW AIRPORT LANDSCAPES

Recent landscape designs for new operating airports and conversions of former airfields and airports into new urban parks and neighborhoods in many cases seek to envision new ideas for future land use and aesthetics while grounding them in their location and its context. In some instances, as with the closed Tempelhofer Feld, parts of the unrealized design and some ideas that govern the newly "found" vast open space seek to create a social utopia. The winning design by GROSS.MAX. as well as the park's

70   Peattie, *Planners and Protesters*, 21.

71   See ibid., 25. For the protest movement against Start-bahn 18 West, see Ralph Nessel and Cornelia Nowak, *Startbahn 18 West: Voraussetzungen und Folgen des Bürgerengagements gegen den Ausbau des Frankfurter Flughafens–Eine Fallstudie* (Frankfurt am Main:

Haag+Herchen Verlag, 1982).

72   See Jean-Marie Charon, *Les mouvements d'opposants aux décisions d'implantation d'aéroports et de aligne nouvelle de T.G.V.* (Paris: Institut d'Urbanisme de l'Académie de Paris, 1979), 6; Peattie, *Planners and Protesters*, 26.

73   See Peattie, *Planners and Protesters*, 28–31; Dorothy Nelkin, *Jetport: The Boston Airport Controversy* (New Brunswick, NJ: Transaction Books, 1974), 47–52, 80–101, 166–170.

74   Peattie, *Planners and Protesters*, 29.

Kurt Schäfer, "village of resistance," or "village of huts" (*Hüttendorf*), built by protesters against Startbahn West in the woods on the grounds of the planned runway at Frankfurt International Airport, October 1980.

Drawings illustrating a design for a shack for an air park made out of logs and local stone, Alabama, 1930s.

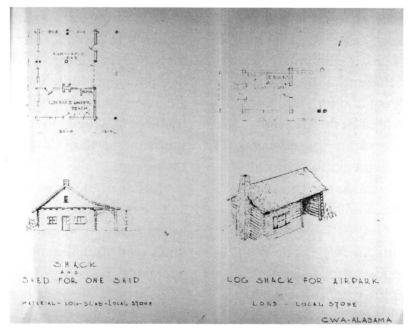

minimally designed current state are the result of numerous citizen petitions and referenda, surveys, workshops, charettes, excursions, and Internet platforms.[75] The collection of ideas for the park has turned the area into a laboratory for urban development that relies on the merging of bottom-up and top-down processes as well as environmental protection. The city government, with the designers, has created a framework and overall vision that depends on citizens' creative potential and entrepreneurial energy—counting on do-it-yourself initiatives and private-public partnerships for the realization of parts of the park and its programming. It considers the park a "platform enabling proactive forms of cultural engagement" that can inspire an active citizenry.[76]

Tempelhofer Feld provides an example of process-oriented urban planning that is meant to anticipate change and embrace the site's evolution. "Pioneer areas," 30- to 47-acre plots of land, can be used on a temporary basis by citizen groups that apply with an idea and are selected by the Tempelhof Project GmbH, a state-owned development agency. Among current uses of the pioneer areas are community gardening, an area used for the building of huts by children, and a school for monocycling. Presenting the city with what some consider an asset and others a burden, Tempelhof has provided Berlin with an open space for testing new planning approaches and ideas. Current planning seeks to activate varied uses of the grounds and explicitly encourages community engagement and activism, as well as nature and species protection, which at the moment are preventing any type of development. In the latest referendum (2014), Berlin's citizens determined that the three areas slated

for urban development at the park's edges should not be developed and that the landscape architects' plan not be carried out, leaving the park the way it is.

Munich boasts one of the earliest airport-park conversions. In the 1960s, the Oberwiesenfeld, Munich's first airfield that had been used in the postwar years to collect the city's rubble, was turned into a sports park that would host the 1972 Olympic Games. The Olympiapark, designed as an "architectural landscape" of flowing forms into which the sports stadia were embedded, was a social laboratory for its landscape designers. Landscape architect Günther Grzimek, whose aim was to serve a democratic pluralistic society, wanted to create a park for an emancipated public free from societal conventions.[77] At a time when German society was building a new democracy after the events of World War II, the park was to provide open space in both a literal and a figurative sense. Grzimek aspired for his design to encourage people to appropriate the spaces for their own uses. His design was to anticipate and therefore enable self-organization. For example, Grzimek argued, the park's landforms and design aesthetic would anticipate where pathways would develop along desire lines. Thus he sought to create a new type of public park in which the aesthetic of flowing land forms functioned as a subtle means to both manipulate and empower the public.

As one of the most well-known landscape architecture firms in Munich, Grzimek's office was later also involved in the landscape plan and design for Munich's most recent airport, which opened in 1992. Given its siting northeast of the city, within a historically and culturally

75   For an analysis and interpretation of airport conversions into parks in general and Tempelhofer Feld in particular, see Dümpelmann, *Flights of Imagination*, chapter 6.

76   Senate Department for Urban Development, *Tempelhof Parkland: Open Landscape Planning Competition Followed by a Negotiated Procedure Invitation to Tender* (Berlin, 2010), 120–121.

77   For Günther Grzimek's design for Olympiapark, see Stefanie Hennecke, Regine Keller, and Juliane Schneegans, eds., *Demokratisches Grün: Olympiapark München* (Berlin: Jovis, 2013).

significant peat bog, the airport's construction did not lack social and environmental opposition. The landscape architects worked hard to turn the airport into "an airport in green" ("Flughafen im Grünen"). On the basis of a regional site analysis that identified characteristic landscape features and elements, Grzimek's firm established that the existing geometric landscape structure based on the local 19th-century peat bog industry and agriculture could accommodate and embed the airport infrastructure.[78] Elements such as rows of trees along drainage canals turned out to be ideal for merging the airport with its surroundings. The firm's seemingly paradoxical design guidelines determined that the airport landscape should be embedded within its agrarian surroundings yet heighten the contrast between the two. The designers sought to achieve this through tree and shrub plantings along an abstract diagonal grid that built upon the bed of the river Isar and was oriented parallel to it. The creation of a geometric cultural landscape also involved bioengineered earthworks along roadsides and bridges that were to have sharp edges, thus defining geometric space or volume.[79]

Although European cities such as Munich and Berlin have been particularly active in converting former airfields and airports into parks—both cities have realized two such projects—the early-20th-century anticipation of American planners that obsolete airports would be turned into parks and integrated into urban park systems has become a global phenomenon in the last 20 years. As the presentation of Airport Afterlives in this book reveals, plans and designs that reenvision airports as new public urban parks have been drawn up in the United States, Canada,

Ecuador, Venezuela, and Taiwan, often following international design competitions. The task of turning vast horizontal grounds into parks and urban neighborhoods is preoccupying many other planning departments worldwide. The global phenomenon of air travel is offering designers opportunities to create new environments that harness and highlight local characteristics and serve local communities. If it has always been an objective at operating airports to welcome passengers through appropriate design, decommissioned airports now offer designers, planners, and in some cases also the public a testing ground for new design ideas and the development of new social utopias. Airports have become the "new urban opportunities" for park building, as parks and arts advocate August Heckscher suggested tentatively in 1977. More often than he could perhaps envision at the time, airports and airfields have since become a windfall.[80]

78   Flughafen München GmbH, ed., *Gestaltungsrichtlinien Flughafen München, Heft 1: Aussenanlagen* (Munich: Hansen Offizin Rotis, 1981), 10.

79   Flughafen München GmbH, *Gestaltungsrichtlinien*.

80   See August Heckscher, *Open Spaces: The Life of American Cities* (New York: Harper & Row, 1977), 214–215.

Airport Afterlives

PRODUCTION

Operating airports are a driving force behind globalization in their capacity as transportation hubs and intermodal nodes for products and goods from all over the world, but what happens when an airport is decommissioned? Food crises, urban food deserts, and other public health concerns have led to many ideas to transform the large open areas of former airfields into sites for urban agriculture and the production of renewable energy.

The conversion of former airports provides designers with the unique opportunity to experiment with new models of public-oriented urban development. Turned into parkland, these sites can create microclimates and enhance the environmental quality of adjacent areas. For example, the winning project for the Taichung Gateway

Park competition converts a decommissioned airport into a weather machine, enticing citizens to spend time outdoors despite the tropical climate with its heavy rainfall and oppressive heat. Some former airfields in Germany, such as the one in Oldenburg, have been turned into solar parks, while in Gatow, near Berlin, the design for the old airfield converts portions of the former runways into agricultural land. This sort of revitalization is taking place in Quito, Ecuador, as well, where a decommissioned field will provide space for urban farming. In Iceland, thermal energy is being considered in a design proposal for the area near the Reykjavík Airport. In this instance, a large server farm underneath a former runway will heat the greenhouses above to produce local fruits and vegetables.

TXG

Taichung Gateway Park, Taichung, Taiwan. Competition 2011.
Mosbach Paysagistes
Philippe Rahm architectes
Ricky Liu Associates

Oblique aerial view of park design.

The former Shueinan Airport, located in downtown Taichung (Taiwan's third-largest city) was originally built by the Japanese army in the 1930s. During World War II, the airfield served as a crucial staging ground for Japan's operations. Shueinan continued to be a military base following the Japanese occupation, but also served commercial domestic flights. In 2004, when the Ching Chuan Kang Air Base expanded, becoming an international commercial airport, Shueinan was decommissioned. In 2007, the municipal government outlined a vision for turning Shueinan into an engine for the city's revitalization and modernization. Following an international design competition, Stan Allen Architect's master plan for a new urban district on the site included a 70-hectare urban park. Taichung's planned "Central Park" was imagined as a large green corridor integrating commercial, residential, and cultural activities.

A design for this green space was the objective of the competition for Taichung Gateway Park that was launched in 2011. The winning design proposal, "Phase Shift Park" by Mosbach Paysagistes and Philippe Rahm architectes, seeks to create an environment that can provide citizens with relief from the tropical heat and humidity, while sheltering them from the noise and air pollution of the city. The project's objective is to mitigate the extreme climate so that the park will be sought out by Taichung's citizens, rather than avoided. Different land formations, varying vegetation, water fountains, atomizers, and electrical devices reduce the heat, humidity, and pollution. Throughout the park, the flow, drainage, and condensation of rainwater are controlled. Plants are used to remediate polluted water and runoff, while wind turbines in the northern area supply the park's energy needs, including electronic devices and lighting.

Perspectival rendering of park areas with elements and devices for climate control.

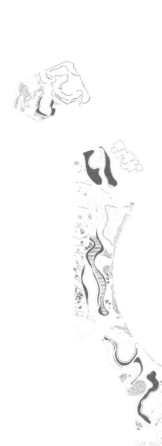

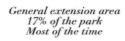

General extension area
17% of the park
Most of the time

Average extension area
25% of the park
Heavy rain

Special extension area
80% of the park
Exceptional event

Perspectival and aerial oblique renderings of various park areas.

Park design.

GWW

Park Landscape and Urban Agriculture Gatow, Gatow, Germany. Competition 2010–2011.
Büro Kiefer Landschaftsarchitektur Berlin

Oblique aerial photograph showing new urban development and the remains of the airfield.

Three years after the withdrawal of the British military from the site, the airfield at Gatow had become obsolete and was closed in 1997. Since then, plans to provide areas for residential development on the former airfield have been realized, and in 2010 and 2011, a competition was held for the design of a public park on large parts of the remaining site.

Büro Kiefer's winning competition design seeks to use and enhance the existing structures and qualities of the site. Traces of the two runways are maintained and mark the transition between the southern and northern parts of the park. The northern runway is to be turned into agricultural land for crop rotation. The park design proposes open lawn areas in the south that include spaces for active sports and other recreational uses. In the north, strips of meadow and grassland parcels alternate with strips of high forbs. Additions to the existing forests in the north and west will create a boundary zone.

Remaining parts of the decommissioned shooting range as well as the earthen ramparts in the northwest of the site will be turned into a climbing wall, a skating rink, and a slide.

In the center of the site, the design proposes the allotment of community gardens for fruit and vegetable production as well as picnic and barbecue areas.

Perspectival rendering, view across the open field toward the west.

UIO

Parque Bicentenario, Quito, Ecuador. Competition 2008.
Ernesto X. Bilbao, Robert A. Sproull, Jr.

Aerial oblique view of design in context.

The conversion of Quito's Mariscal Sucre International Airport into the Parque Bicentenario officially began this year and will continue throughout the next decade. The decommissioned airport has left a 3.2-kilometer-long clearing within a densely populated metropolis, surrounded by volcanic mountains and sheer cliffs.

The design and planning strategy reestablishes a humid forest, a prairie, and a transitional zone (three unique ecologies that previously converged at this site), and weaves a variety of programs into those ecosystems. The park design builds on two objectives: To reinforce localized site configurations and to avoid dead-end streets at the perimeter by extending them through the park as pedestrian paths. The resulting grid establishes parcels for a variety of crops that showcase Ecuadorean agriculture. Beyond yielding a harvest, these crops help to produce greater public awareness of the nation's farming industry and culture. Parque Bicentenario's enormous scale is comparable to New York's Central Park and enables the project to provide the people of Quito with a wide range of activities. The design proposes that visitors walk through a forest or along a prairie, learn about local and national farming, visit museums, study Ecuadorean plants and animals, and/or take a moment to simply enjoy the vastness of the newly recovered landscape in an otherwise bustling metropolis.

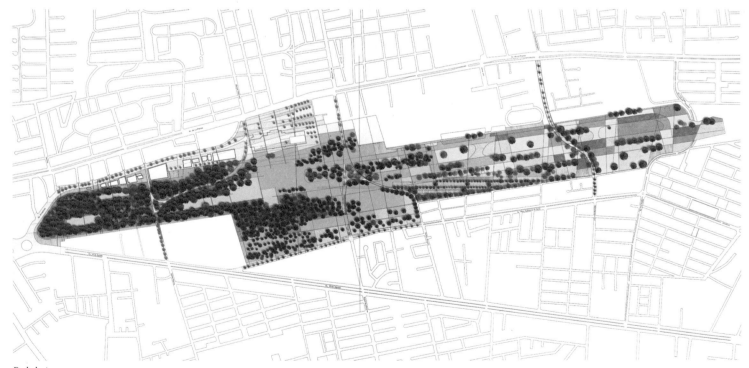

Park design.

RKV

Reykjavík Airport, Vatnsmýri, Iceland. Competition 2007.
Lateral Office

Oblique aerial view of design in context.

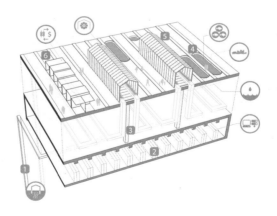

Axonometric detail of production strip, geothermal diagram.

The airport that occupied the Vatnsmýri area, near the center of Reykjavík, Iceland, since the beginning of World War II has closed, and the site is under consideration for new urban development. An international competition was held in 2007 to produce ideas. The Toronto-based firm, Lateral Office, proposed a design "From Runways to Greenways" that uses landscape and exterior programs as a catalyst for urban development. The proposal emphasizes the programming of the open space that connects the urban neighborhoods designed for this new part of the city.

Three runways were converted into greenways, each possessing distinctively different qualities. The east-west greenway is a landscape designed as an extension of the dense forests of Öskjuhlíd Hill, connecting them to the water's edge in the west. The greenway includes fish and tree farms, greenhouses for fruit, vegetable, and flower production, as well as allotment gardens and markets. A computer server farm located below ground generates heat for the greenhouses above. The north-south greenway with its wetlands and hills connects to the ecology of the Hljómskálagardur Park and Lake, and the Nauthólsvík thermal beach to the south. The northeast-southwest greenway is designed as a recreation corridor for four new Vatnsmýri neighborhoods and provides a variety of spaces for sports and other recreational activities. These runway conversions are thought to initiate the development and transformation of the Vatnsmýri area from a place of transportation to a place of recreation, learning, and production.

Park design in context.

EDNO

Oldenburg Airbase Solar Farm, Oldenburg, Germany, 2011.
IFE Eriksen AG.

Oblique aerial photograph of solar park.

Since 2011, solar panels have replaced the German and British fighter planes that once took off from the runways of the 29-hectare former airbase near Oldenburg, Germany. The site in Alexanderheide was first used as a sports airfield in 1933. After its use by the German Luftwaffe during World War II, the British Royal Air Force used it from 1951 to 1957. The site was then given back to the German military until it was decommissioned and cleared in 2008.

In its place, IFE Eriksen AG built the Oldenburg Airbase Solar Farm, with 59,100 solar panels that produce 13 million kilowatt-hours of electricity every year—enough to supply the electricity needs of about 3,200 four-person households. The solar farm is the outgrowth of Germany's political commitment to sustainable development, with a focus on renewable energy and energy efficiency, and an ultimate goal of diminishing dependence on fossil fuels and nuclear power.

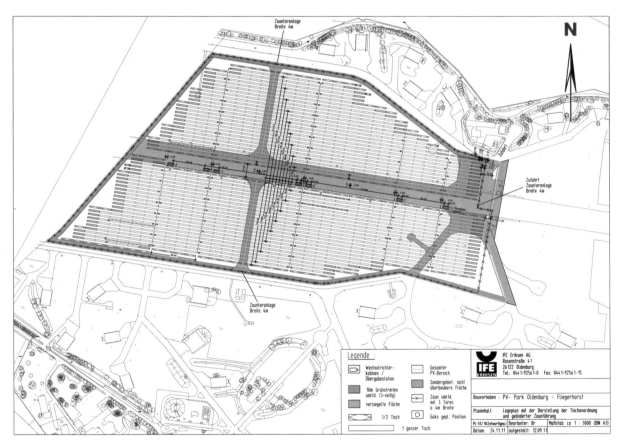

Plan.

Ground views.

Airport Afterlives

Although airport revitalizations offer a great number of benefits, and the conversion of former airports has provided designers with the opportunity to experiment with new models for urban development and the public realm, the expansive terrain of these airfields also comes with challenges. The recuperation of these areas has turned voids in the urban fabric into catalysts for social life and urban development, yet the enormity of these sites often presents difficulties for their adaptation and reuse. The designs featured in this section try to engage citizens and the public in the shaping of the future urban landscape.

At Berlin's former Tempelhof Airport, a form of "temporary urbanism" is being practiced where citizens have been invited to propose provisional uses for predetermined plots on the field. At the former Norwegian international airport, Fornebu (near Oslo), a new urban district is held together by a new community center and a chain of water bodies that form the spine of the district's park space. Similarly, the site of the old international airport in Munich, Germany, has been turned into a new urban neighborhood with a large park that draws people from other parts of the city. Comparable plans exist for the Reykjavík Airport in Iceland and for the airport in the Anfa district of Casablanca, Morocco. Plans to close the military air base in the center of Caracas, Venezuela, have led to a design proposal that aims to create a park for all people from around the city, regardless of their socioeconomic backgrounds. In New York City, Floyd Bennett Field features a campground, community gardens, and educational programs, making it a playground for the entire city.

THF

Berlin Tempelhof Airport, Berlin, Germany. Competition 2010.
GROSS.MAX.
Sutherland Hussey Architects

Oblique aerial view of design in context.

Perspectival rendering of the "crack garden" near one of the park entrances on Columbiadamm.

Established in 1923, Tempelhof Airport in Berlin has played an influential role in aviation history. By the 1930s, it had become one of the world's busiest commercial airports. In 1935, the architect Ernst Sagebiel was commissioned by the Reich Aviation Ministry to draw new plans for an expanded airport. Envisioning a capacity of up to six million passengers a year, he designed the monumental arc-shaped building that is over 1,200 meters long and still stands today. Sagebiel's airport created a gateway to the Nazi empire in Albert Speer's vision for the city. After World War II, Tempelhof was occupied and used by the American military. During the Soviet Union's blockade of the Western sectors of Berlin in 1948 and 1949, Tempelhof played an important role for the airlift. Aircraft carrying thousands of tons of food and provisions flew in and out of Tempelhof, and the airport remained a powerful symbol throughout the Cold War. In 1993, after reunification, the US Air Force handed over the airport to the Berlin Airport Authority.

After its closure to commercial air traffic in 2008, Tempelhof Airport was opened to the public as parkland in 2010. GROSS.MAX.'s 2011 winning competition design for the transformation and development of this open space envisions a 380-hectare public urban park. The design aims to retain the character of the site while offering a space for a wide range of new activities. It capitalizes on the urban panorama and the sky above Berlin ("Himmel über Berlin") that the wide, open space offers. The design promotes the notion of "nature activation"—that is,

it seeks not only to conserve biodiversity but also to enhance it. It also builds on a Berlin-specific form of temporary urbanism in which so-called urban pioneers—entrepreneurial citizens—are allowed to occupy parts of the site and become active agents in its transformation.

The design incorporates overlapping paths that orbit around the two parallel runways connecting the planned urban neighborhoods surrounding the park. New bodies of water recycle the runoff from the existing 28 hectares of hard surface and the roofs of the former terminal building. A 40-meter-high rock monument that houses an interior climbing school, dedicated to Alexander von Humboldt, acts as a landmark on the vast horizontal plane. On the metropolitan scale, the design provides an unprecedented outdoor living room and events area for Berlin. On the neighborhood scale, it offers small parks and gardens along the edge and at the entrance areas.

Perspectival rendering of the park panorama looking across water basin toward former terminal building.

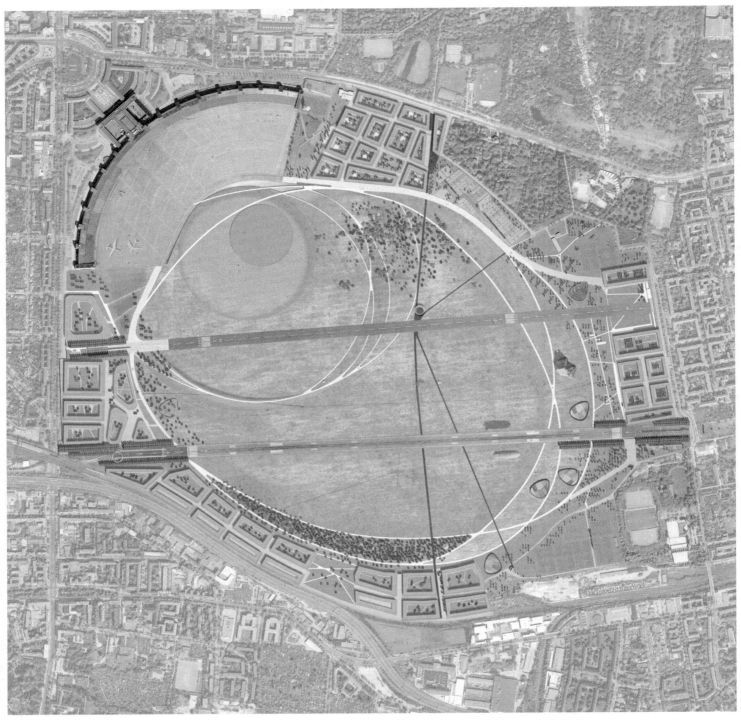

Park design in context.

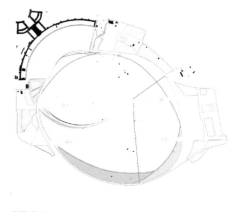

PHASE 1. Pioneers

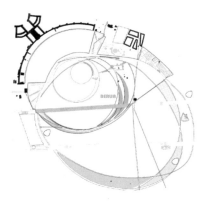

PHASE 2. IGA

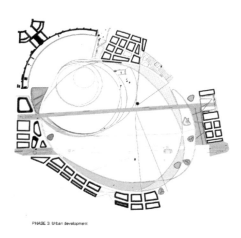

PHASE 3. Urban development

Phasing of the pioneer use strategy.

Rock monument.

FBU

Oslo Airport, Fornebu, Oslo, Norway. 2004–2008.
Bjørbekk & Lindheim Landskapsarkitekter
Atelier Dreiseitl (water artist and consultant)

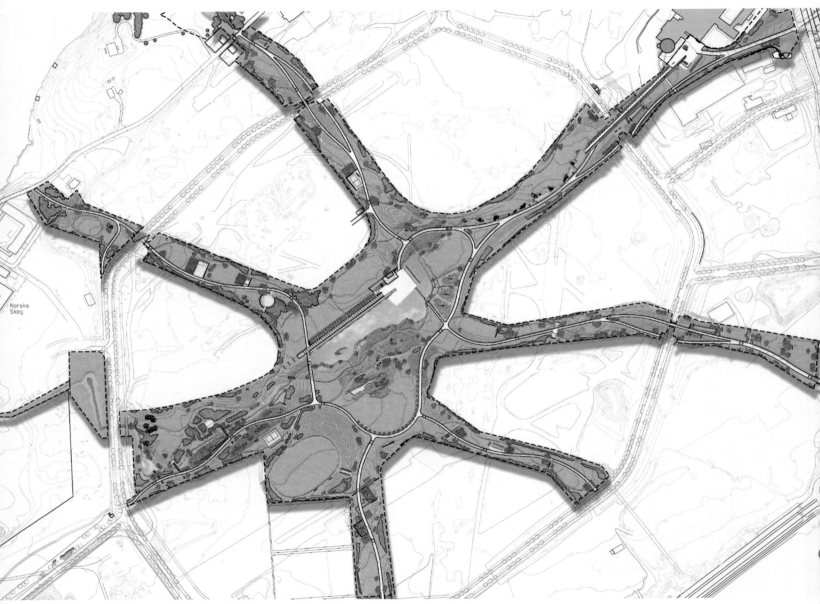

Park design in context.

The environmental remediation and conversion of Oslo's former international airport into a new urban neighborhood with 6,000 housing units and workspaces for 15,000 people resulted in one of the largest industrial reclamation projects in the country. The park forms a functional focus and an identifying centerpiece for the new community, which is located 10 kilometers from downtown Oslo. The park has been designed as a link between the uncompromising linearity of the former airport and the softer, more organic forms of the preexisting landscape. Seven park "arms" between 30 and 100 meters wide include meeting places and activity areas that stretch out into the new neighborhood from the park's central spine.

The former terminal building and control tower marks the starting point for a central water feature that stretches from north to south through the park. The design of the waterway creates the experience of water flowing in streams, falling in cascades and fountains, and forming a still surface in reflecting pools. A plaza, or multipurpose floor with large slabs of stone and moveable water elements, invites children to manipulate the flowing streams. A large amphitheater provides a space for various kinds of performances, as well as for quiet reflection.

Oblique aerial photograph of the site before the airport conversion.

Oblique aerial photograph taken shortly after construction of the park began.

MUC

Landscape Park Munich-Riem, Germany. 1995–2006.
Latitude Nord

Oblique aerial photograph.

Closed in 1992, the site of the former Munich-Riem Airport has been turned into a new urban district, which includes a convention center and a new park that covers 200 hectares south of the new urban development. The park design is based on Latitude Nord's winning entry in an international design competition held in 1995.

The park provides a 400-meter-wide band of open space that enables airflow between the large forests in the east and the city center, supplying downtown Munich with cooler air in the summer. The diagonal layout and the orientation of the gridded groves of trees that are characteristic of the site—such as hornbeam, pine, and oak—support this climate function. They also build on the orientation of vernacular field patterns in the area. In some locations, the trees are planted as gridded blocks and groves, whereas in other areas they align more loosely, imitating the hedgerows delineating the surrounding agricultural fields. These plantings create a variety of spaces and atmospheres, and alternate with open flowering meadows. A large lake can be used for swimming. Carefully contoured landforms provide views of the downtown and the Alps beyond, and also offer opportunities for winter sledding.

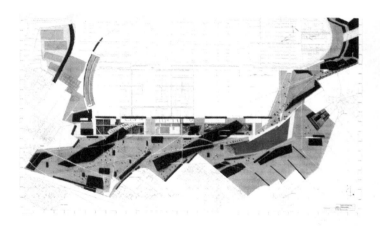

Park design.

Oblique aerial photograph of gridded tree plantations.

LA CARLOTA

Generalísimo Francisco de Miranda Air Base, La Carlota, Caracas, Venezuela. Competition 2012.
Anita Berrizbeitia et al.

Oblique aerial view of park design.

LA CARLOTA

The Francisco de Miranda military air base (Aeropuerto La Carlota) occupies 103 hectares in the center of Caracas, adjacent to Roberto Burle Marx's Parque del Este. A 2012 design competition generated ideas for its conversion into a park. The design focuses on the park as a place where a divided society can share experiences within the context of sports and cultural events. The simple design can be realized quickly, should political conditions become more propitious for the construction of a public space of this scale. It reconfigures the runway into a programmatic spine for the location of stadia, markets, swimming pools, and music shells. A landform along the northern park edge shields the highway, recycles materials from demolition, retains storm water, and offers elevated paths along its crest, seating on its slopes, and landing areas for the bridges that provide access to the park from the north. A field of *chaguaramo* palms extends across the park, giving it a distinct identity. Referencing Parque del Este to the north, groves of flowering trees emblematic of Caracas, including *Acacia* and *Araguaney*, are to bloom sequentially, forming drifts of brilliant colors under the palms. Plazas of varied size located throughout the park are connected by a system of pathways that include cycling and jogging trails.

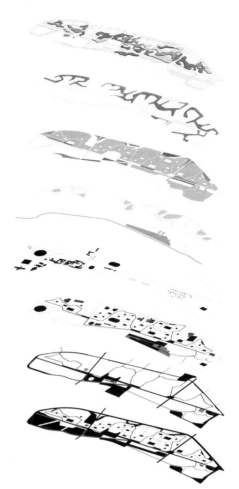

Layer diagram: vegetation, topography, soft surfaces, hydrology, buildings, programs, circulation, hard surfaces.

Oblique aerial view across the lake.

CAS

Anfa Airport, Casablanca, Morocco. Commenced 2007.
Agence Ter
Reichen et Robert & Associés

Oblique aerial view of the airstrip.

Perspectival rendering showing an aerial view of the envisioned central park.

The 450-hectare site of the former airport located in the Anfa district is being turned into a new cultural and business zone for the city. The site will house a business center including office space, private residences, a new university, an aeronautical museum, and a theater. Agence Ter and Reichen & Robert's design for the former airport site seeks to preserve the horizon of the old runway and emphasize existing and newly created sightlines toward the sea and the Hassan II Mosque.

The center of the design for the Anfa district is a 50-hectare park adjacent to the disused runway. Strips of woods including *Acacia* and *Gleditsia* alternate with flowered prairies in the park. Its western sections are made up of gardens planted with hydrophilic varieties that collect rainwater and make maximum use of rainy periods in the Mediterranean climate. The flat runways and taxiways are interspersed with open plots of land that offer the possibility of reestablishing natural habitats. Agence Ter is creating a park that is the engine for new urban development in this part of the city.

Landscape design for the new Anfa district.

Perspectival rendering of the wetland.

RKV

Vatnsmýri, Reykjavík, Iceland. Competition 2007.
Graeme Massie Architects

Aerial view showing the closed-down airport.

The Vatnsmýri area near the center of Reykjavík has been the site of an airport since the beginning of World War II. The site of the former airport is now under consideration for further urban development. An international competition was held in 2007 to produce ideas. Graeme Massie Architects' winning proposal, "Reciprocity: The Shaping of a Capital City," sees the projected closure of the airport and the development of the Vatnsmýri area as an opportunity to further strengthen Reykjavík's identity and reputation as an international destination attractive to residents, tourists, and businesses. The design proposes an urban expansion that is economically, socially, and environmentally sustainable and is closely connected with the existing infrastructure and urban fabric of the city center. It also plans to build on the spatial relationships and sightlines between the historic city center, lake, waterfront, hill, and landmarks such as Hallgrímskirkja Church and the City Hall, to create a new, recognizably distinct district that is both urban in character and closely linked to the landscape. New park areas become a unifying element connecting the city center with the new district.

Urban design in context.

Diagram highlighting the different neighborhoods.

DEN

Stapleton Redevelopment, Denver, Colorado. Commenced 1997.
AECOM

Stapleton Greenway Park looking west toward downtown Denver.

Sections of Westerly Creek "before" (as Stapleton International Airport runway) and "after" (as restored creek).

After Stapleton International Airport closed in 1995, plans to integrate the former airport lands into Denver's urban fabric began to take shape. After contamination remediation, one of the largest master-planned communities in the country was built on the 1,900-hectare site. The design guidelines developed by the private, non-profit Stapleton Development Foundation asked for the new urban development to follow a New Urbanist vision that emphasizes "defined centers for services and civic uses, walkable scale, access to nearby employment, diverse transportation options, and strong connections to parks and nature." Several firms contributed to the master plan, including Cooper, Robertson and Partners; Calthorpe Associates; and AECOM (formerly EDAW), which has also provided guidelines, master plans, and designs for neighborhood parks, streetscapes, greenways, and other open space infrastructure such as amphitheaters, pools, and squares. This open space, which makes up 30 percent of the entire area, is an integral component of the urban infill project. It is a mixed-use community with neo-historicist homes planned for 25,000 residents and 30,000 jobs. The airport's control tower has been maintained as a landmark for the neighborhood.

Westerly Creek looking west toward Central Park and preserved control tower.

NOP

Floyd Bennett Field
National Park Service
Ashley Scott Kelly and Rikako Wakabayashi

Oblique aerial photograph.

Floyd Bennett Field was first used as an airfield in the 1920s and was dedicated as New York's first municipal airport in 1931. It was turned over to the Navy in 1941 and transferred to the National Park Service in 1972. Located in the southeast corner of the New York City borough of Brooklyn, it was built on fill within a tidal estuary and bound by water on three sides. More than 200,000 people live within 4.8 kilometers of the park. The region expects 3.8 million new residents by 2030, and the field's 550 hectares are expected to fulfill some of the future need for open park space. The park currently functions as a public venue for a variety of recreational pursuits, including model plane flying, land sailing, biking, and camping. Brooklyn's largest community garden is located on the former airfield, and the site offers outdoor sports fields, indoor ice rinks, and sports facilities such as a rock-climbing wall and courts for ball games.

The winning design in the 2007 competition for the entire Gateway National Recreation Area, sponsored by the Van Alen Institute, the National Parks Conservation Association, and Columbia University and entitled "Mapping the Ecotone," suggests maintaining the current uses and the old runways. The design by Ashley Scott Kelly and Rikako Wakabayashi proposes elevated pathways, as well as piers and jetties that take into account projected sea level rise and the site's vulnerability to storm surges. The design "Reassembling Ecologies" by North Design Office that won second prize envisioned a stronger definition of programs and activities that would be moved toward the Flatbush Avenue side of the park, allowing for the rest of the field to be returned to "nature," promoting nature observation and environmental education programs.

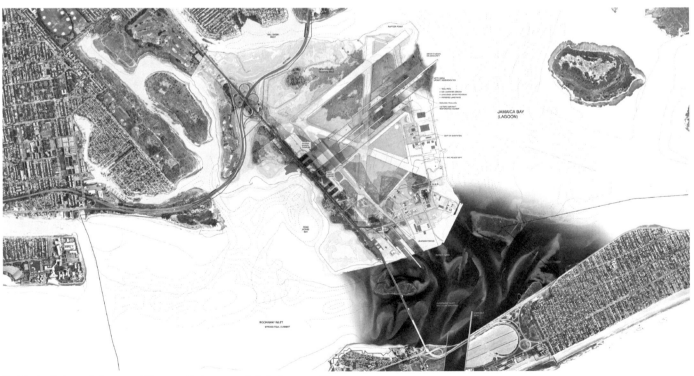

Envisioning Gateway design competition 2007. Design proposal of winning competition entry by Ashley Scott Kelly and Rikako Wakabayashi "Mapping the Ecotone."

Airport Afterlives

SUCCESSION

Design projects for former airfields and airports have played a key role in recent developments in landscape architecture. Decommissioned fields have given designers, city governments, and developers new and, until now, unforeseen opportunities, providing grounds for experimentation with old and new theories of ecological succession. The exceptional environmental conditions that former airfields possess—with their dry, compacted, contaminated soils and their unobstructed exposure to weather—have paradoxically turned many of them into havens for endangered species. The vastness of these sites has also led to numerous conversion proposals that assume the character of development frameworks and transformation strategies, rather than designs that locate specific programs and determine particular forms and materials.

The proposals for Downsview Park in Toronto emphasize the importance of temporal change, self-organization, and indeterminacy in landscape architecture. In contrast, the core of the Landscape Park Johannisthal in Berlin is an inaccessible nature reserve and habitat of endangered species in which succession is arrested through a maintenance regimen of a flock of sheep. The proposal for Berlin's former Tempelhof Airport provides a design framework for the park's spontaneous appropriation by citizens and visitors, while the former Harvard Airfield in Quincy, Massachusetts, has been transformed into Squantum Point Park by fostering ecological succession and the reestablishment of tidal marshland.

YZD

Downsview Park, Toronto, Canada. Competition 1999.
Bernard Tschumi Architects
Gunta Mackars

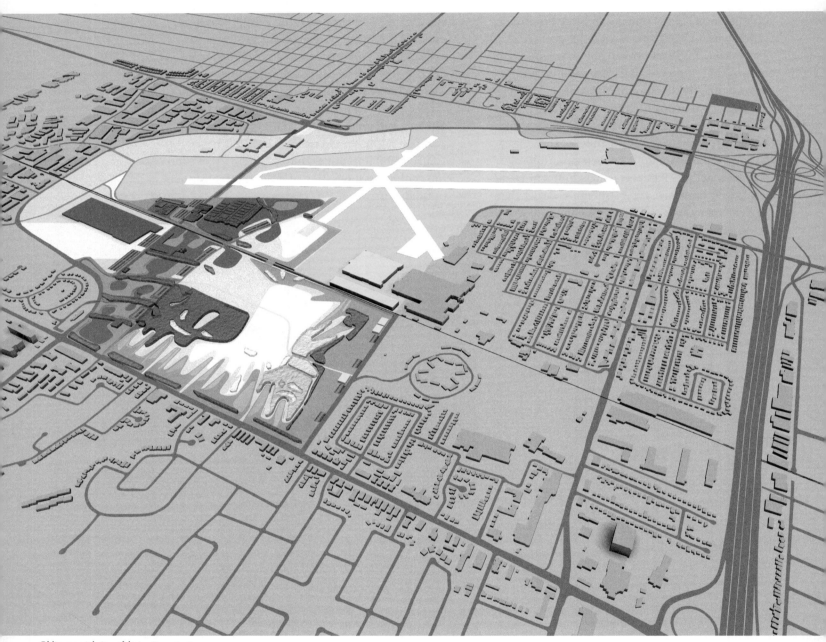

Oblique aerial view of design in context.

Aircraft construction and test flights by de Havilland Aircraft Company of Canada began at the Downsview site on the outskirts of Toronto in 1929 and expanded throughout the 1930s. Downsview Airport was established as a military air base in the 1940s. Situated on a high point in the landscape, with expansive views to downtown, the site was eventually engulfed by the expanding city. When the Canadian government decommissioned Downsview in 1994, it decided to turn the site into the country's first urban national park. Stakeholders emphasized the need for a park that would reconcile the site's history with contemporary recreational uses, while also regenerating biodiversity, ground water, and other eroded natural systems. As a consequence, the 1999 design competition for Toronto's Downsview Park on the 129-hectare site of the obsolete military airstrip (though still being used by Bombardier/de Havilland for test flights) asked for the development of a new landscape that combined public use with the establishment and conservation of wildlife, and the protection of natural systems. The park had to integrate the airstrip and existing military sheds large enough to accommodate soccer fields or major movie sets. Situated on a topographical divide between two large watersheds, the park would require a plan that responded to the logic of flows.

The conceptual idea for the park design by Bernard Tschumi Architects builds on the notion that in the 21st century, every place is "urban," even in the middle of the "wilderness." Airstrips, information centers, public performance spaces, and the Internet require a redefinition of parks and nature. Therefore the design confronts two realities—the digital and the wild, or (in homage to the lonely prairie wolf found barking during an early morning site visit) the digital and "the coyote"—and seeks to merge them. The design strategy is "to maximize, attract, and seduce." The presence and length of the perimeter is maximized, increasing the interface between natural and cultural artifacts. The industrial military buildings are spools to attract events and sports activities. Large screens made of photographic fabric or electronic devices are attached to the buildings at various intervals. These elements are the major physical and spatial means for defining and activating the park. Time, rather than space, is to become the main agent of the project.

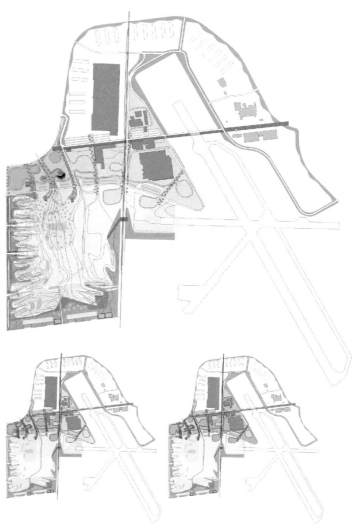

Plans showing the phases of development.

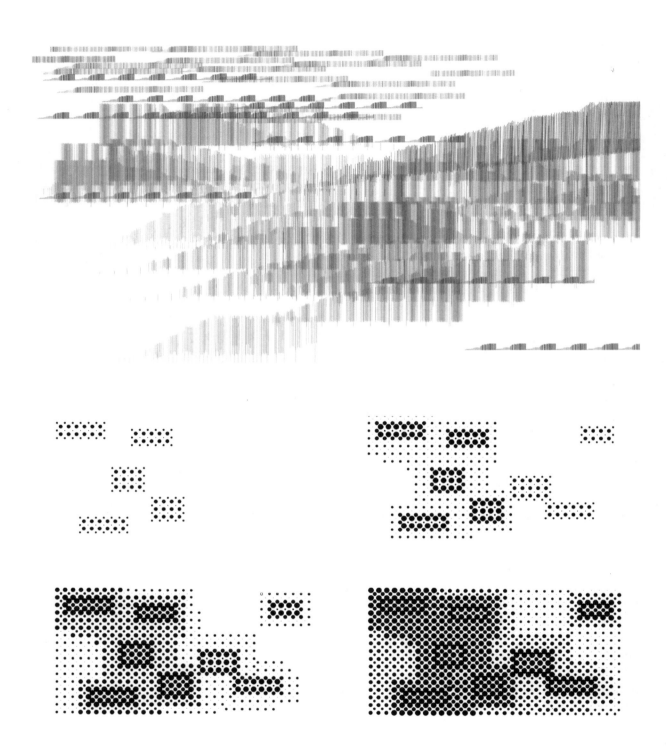

Diagrams illustrating the establishment and succession of mixed wood forest.

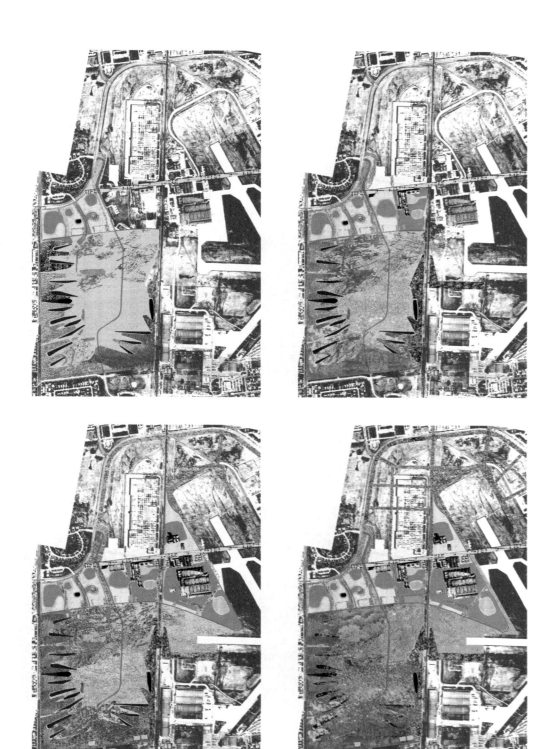

Collages illustrating the succession of vegetation: five years spring, 10 years fall,
15 years spring, 30 years fall.

JOHANNISTHAL

Landscape Park Johannisthal, Berlin, Germany. 1996; construction 1998–2010.
Büro Kiefer Landschaftsarchitektur Berlin

Oblique aerial photograph of the park and new urban development.

Located southeast of Berlin's city center on the site of one of Germany's first airfields, the Landscape Park Johannisthal provides an expansive green open core for the new district of Adlershof, currently still under development. Having been vacant for decades after World War II, the former airfield became home to many endangered species and was declared a nature conservation area in 2003. The park design creates a spatial framework and accommodates both nature conservation and recreation. It consists of three park areas that vary in character and public accessibility. The nature conservation area forms the core of the park that is not accessible; it is maintained by a flock of sheep that graze on the dry grassland during the day and are penned outside the nature park at night. An elevated promenade and viewing platforms retained by gabions circumscribe the nature conservation area and mark the transition to the park areas that can be used for active sports, other recreational activities, and playgrounds. The uses in these areas were not determined in the initial plan, so that the park development is able to react flexibly to the needs of citizens. At the three corners of the park, wooded areas mark the entrances and provide a contrast to the expansive meadows that make up most of its grounds.

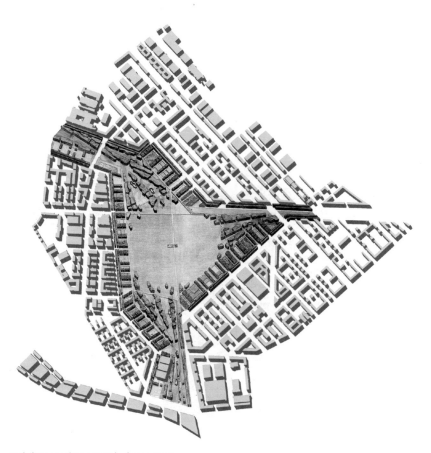

Park design in the projected urban context.

Collage illustrating one of the park platforms.

Collage illustrating a space for recreational activities and individual garden plots along the park edges.

Views into the nature reserve from the surrounding elevated promenade.

THF

Berlin Tempelhof Airport, Berlin, Germany. Competition 2010.
Topotek 1
Dürig AG

Perspectival rendering showing an oblique aerial view of the design.

Park design in context.

After its closure to commercial air traffic in 2008, Tempelhof Airport was opened to the public as parkland in 2010. The design proposal by Topotek 1 and Dürig AG is based on a layering of uses and of old and new structures, with the aim of maintaining the airfield's original character and qualities. A tree-lined promenade circum-scribes the field and connects the areas that are given over temporarily to citizens—so-called urban pioneers—for their free use in the bound-ary zone. It forms an area of transition between the planned urban neighborhoods adjacent to the field and the open field, or "urban savanna." It offers seating opportunities and small spaces to socialize and view the panorama of the former airfield from underneath a protective tree canopy. The network of paths across the expansive open field reflects the system of triangulated flight paths in airspace. A grid of crosses overlays the field, marking potential locations of platforms for informal programs, spontaneous events, meeting places, and belvederes. Gridded oak groves known as "tree archipelagos" are scattered throughout the field. They provide orientation and scale comparisons. The runways are main-tained and turned into tracks for a variety of sports including biking and kite skating. The taxiway offers space for food trucks, mobile libraries, and play facilities, while areas in the south of the field are proposed for urban agriculture.

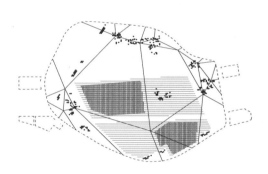

Diagram, bird habitats, trees, and open grassland.

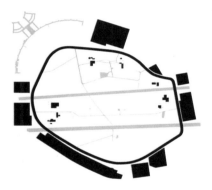

Diagram, areas for "urban pioneers."

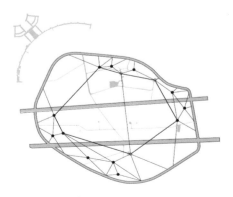

Diagram, main pathways, and points of activity.

YZD

Downsview Park, Toronto, Canada. Competition 1999.
James Corner Field Operations
Stan Allen Architect
Michael Horsham, Tomato

Oblique aerial photograph, 2013.

The design competition for Toronto's Downsview Park on the site of an obsolete military airstrip, still used by Bombardier Dash 8 aircraft (a.k.a. de Havilland Canada Dash 8) for test flights, asked for the development of a new landscape that combined public use with the establishment and conservation of wildlife, and the protection of natural systems. The design proposal "Emergent Ecologies" by James Corner Field Operations and Stan Allen Architect proposes a framework for the development of new natural and cultural life on the site. It seeks to facilitate processes of self-organization. The design consists of an overlay of two complementary organizational strategies: "Circuit Ecologies," consisting of circuitous pathways with event spaces and active programs, and "Through-Flow Ecologies," made up of habitats, plantings, drainage systems, and infrastructure such as lighting and informational markers. The design framework is intended to respond flexibly to the unforeseeable future developments of the site's natural systems and cultural programs.

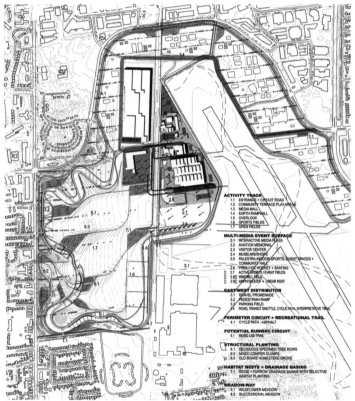

Park design in context.

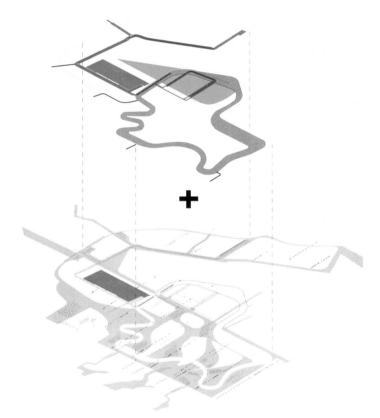

Layer diagram illustrating "Circuit Ecologies" and "Through-Flow Ecologies."

SQUANTUM

Squantum Point Park, Quincy, Massachusetts, United States. 1997–2001.
Carol R. Johnson Associates

Oblique aerial photograph.

Squantum Point Park is a 17.4-hectare parcel of land along Boston Harbor for which Carol R. Johnson Associates (CRJA) prepared a master plan in 1999, as well as a full design for a 1.8-hectare Phase I Improvements Plan in 2000. Developed by the Department of Conservation and Recreation of the Commonwealth of Massachusetts, the Phase I improvements were completed and the park opened to the public in 2001. The park is located on the former Harvard Aviation Field that was used by the Harvard Aeronautical Society from 1910 until 1917 as a site for the first Harvard-Boston aviation meets. Subsequently turned into the Squantum Naval Air Station by the US Navy, the airfield was closed in the 1950s. Since the 1980s, parts of the area have been turned into a New Urbanist residential neighborhood.

The master plan for the waterfront park was laid out to maintain bird habitats and traces of the site's aviation history. The plan's park facilities include a boat launch, parking, a soccer field, and pedestrian esplanades that enhance public access to the waterfront. Working with waterfront engineers, CRJA developed solutions for shoreline stabilization and salt marsh wetland replication using sustainable methods such as bioengineering wherever feasible. Pathways outline one of the runways. Historical and environmental markers along the primary pathway called the "flight path" inform visitors about the site's history and ecology. All new park facilities are designed to enhance the site's wetlands and natural wildlife habitat. A lookout point was constructed at the northernmost tip of the site to enable views of Dorchester Bay, Logan Airport, the Neponset River Estuary, and the downtown Boston skyline.

Interpretive marker.

The point overlook looking north toward UMass Boston and the Boston skyline.

Airport Afterlives

TOPOGRAPHY

Airfields have been engineered to reduce biological and hydrological processes. Since the characteristics of these sites include their large size, openness, and horizontality, many designers have interpreted airfields as blank slates for topographic and hydrological invention and intervention. Cut and fill, insertions, and landforms have been prominent in the work of many landscape architects on airport sites. These practices are often used in connection with the daylighting of streams and creeks, the re-creation of wildlife habitats, and the implementation of extensive water systems.

The design for Hellinikon Metropolitan Park on the site of the former international airport in Athens, Greece, is based on topographic modification of water collection and retention. Proposals for the conversion of the former international airport in Quito, Ecuador, foresee the creation of lakes to collect water from the surrounding mountains. In the tropical climate of Taichung, Taiwan, where water is paradoxically still in short supply, the park is envisioned as an enormous water treatment infrastructure. At Orange County Great Park near Irvine, California, streams and creeks are daylighted to provide the structure for the park design, while the former airfield in Novato on San Francisco Bay, California, is being flooded and restored as a wetland.

ATH

Hellinikon Metropolitan Park and Urban Development, Athens. Competition 2005.
Philippe Coignet/Office of Landscape Morphology
Elena Fernandez & David Serero Architects
Erwin Redl (artist)

Oblique aerial view of design in context.

Hellinikon Metropolitan Park and Urban Development is located on the coast of the Mediterranean, 20 kilometers outside of Athens. The airport, built in 1938, was used as a Luftwaffe air base throughout the Nazi occupation of Greece. From 1945 to 1993, it was an operations node for the US Air Force; starting in 1956, however, it served mostly commercial air traffic. The airport closed in 2001, but the iconic East Terminal, designed in 1960 by Eero Saarinen and Associates, remains on the site. The northwest corner of the defunct airport was used in the summer of 2004 to accommodate the Olympic games. In an effort to reclaim the abandoned site as a green space for 21st-century Athens, the International Union of Architects, the Greek Ministry of Environment, and the Organization for the Planning and Environmental Protection of Athens sponsored an open international competition for the design of a new urban park and neighborhood on the 550-hectare site. The brief called for a large urban park with new housing, office space, and civic infrastructure.

The winning landscape design is based on processes of rainwater collection and topographic modification. A series of six corridors, each of which are 200 to 300 meters in width, links the city to the coastline 60 meters below. These corridors of cultivated soil, or softscapes, include a new drainage system and a network of roads, bicycle paths, and walkways that structure the new residential and commercial development.

The softscape corridors use planting and storm-water management to catch, store, and release rainwater through a system of terraces, embankments, and retaining walls that create level ground for various activities. One of the two main airport runways is maintained as a visual and circulation axis running perpendicular to the six softscape corridors. The second and shorter runway extends toward the sea to form an expansive belvedere. The tree-planting strategy responds to the ground and slope conditions, and to the Mediterranean climate. A first plant formation (garrigue) is intended to colonize the internal part of the softscapes, preparing the ground for succession and future mature trees (pine, olive, and oak).

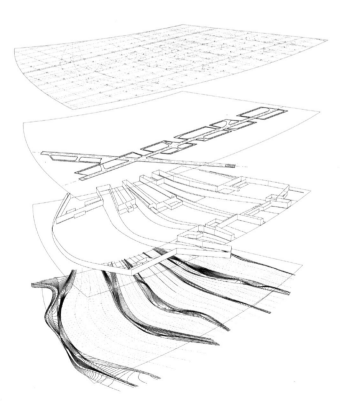

Axonometric drawings of the main structural elements on site.

Park design in context.

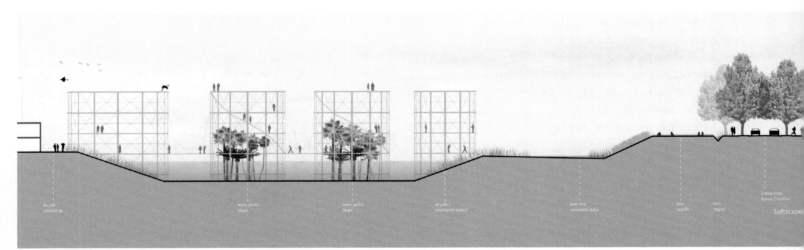

Sections through softscape #3 and softscape #5.

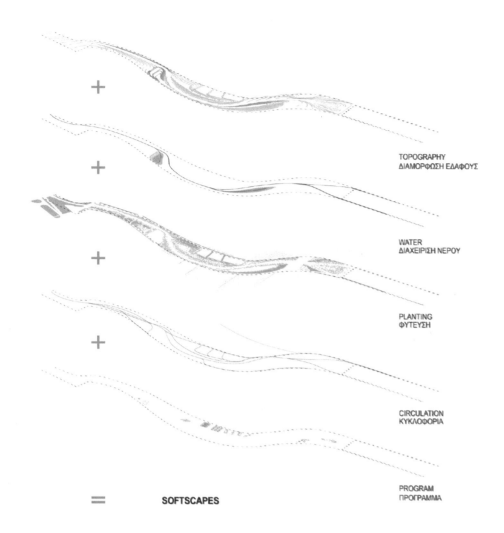

+

+
                                                         TOPOGRAPHY
                                                         ΔΙΑΜΟΡΦΩΣΗ ΕΔΑΦΟΥΣ

+
                                                         WATER
                                                         ΔΙΑΧΕΙΡΙΣΗ ΝΕΡΟΥ

+
                                                         PLANTING
                                                         ΦΥΤΕΥΣΗ

                                                         CIRCULATION
                                                         ΚΥΚΛΟΦΟΡΙΑ

=   **SOFTSCAPES**
                                                         PROGRAM
                                                         ΠΡΟΓΡΑΜΜΑ

Softscape #5 - SECTION AA'

UIO

Mariscal Sucre International Airport, Quito, Ecuador, 2008.
Anita Berrizbeitia et al.

Perspectival renderings of various park areas.

The park design builds upon the topographical location of the former airport site in a valley by proposing the establishment of 34 water bodies. The lakes collect and filter water from the surrounding mountains and also function as wading and swimming pools, fishing ponds, and reflecting basins. Twelve hills throughout the park recall the landforms of Andean glaciers: U-shaped valleys, *cirques*, and *arêtes*. This topographic system performs several functions: 1) It directs and contains water, and generates microclimates; 2) It recycles material from the demolition of the runway and other airport infrastructure; 3) It creates various spaces; and 4) It offers overviews across the longitudinal axes of the valley. A large open oval-shaped area located at the center of the park accommodates big cultural events, and the park's edges are turned into *zócalos*, areas for urban development that include a boundary promenade, as well as public space for cultural programs. Within the park, forested areas, agricultural plots, and gardens alternate and follow a humidity gradient ranging from dry and open areas in the north to wet and densely vegetated areas in the south.

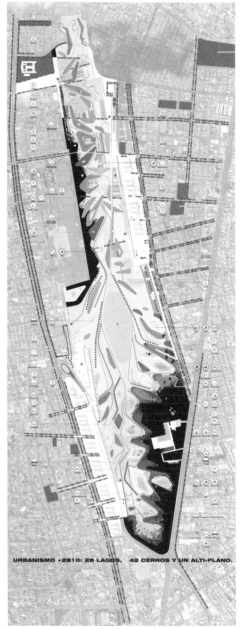

Park design in context.

UIO

Mariscal Sucre International Airport, Quito, Ecuador, 2008.
Paisajes Emergentes

View along the lake from the Aquatic Park.

By flooding the runway of the old airport, the design for "Lake Park" aims to generate an active hydrologic park. The transformation of the runway into an urban park is an opportunity to test the insertion of leisure activities and aquatic ecosystems typical to the tropics. Serving as an impervious platform for a series of linked aquatic interventions, the 3,120-meter runway would be composed of outdoor rooms, designed to have a distinct programmatic character ranging from an open-air aquarium to thermal baths. Thus the linear landscape of events can be understood as a giant hydric machine made up of smaller habitable parts. Nine lakes treat the residual water of the park and nearby buildings. An excavated open-air aquarium is filled with partially processed water from the wetlands. Water from the aquarium that contains organic material is used to fertilize an aquatic botanical garden. A conventional treatment plant oxygenates and filters water from the botanical garden and removes organic material. This clean water fills public pools and thermal baths that are heated with the help of wind and solar energy. Finally, water is collected from a recreational lake and used for irrigation systems and general park maintenance.

Park design in context.

Perspectival rendering of the aquarium.

Longitudinal section through the entire lake.

Perspectival rendering of the amphitheater and water basin for rainwater collection.

TXG

Taichung Gateway Park, Taichung, Taiwan. Competition 2011.
Stoss Landscape Urbanism

Oblique aerial view of design in context.

Stan Allen Architect's design for a new urban quarter on the site of the former Taichung Airport included a large urban park on 70 hectares. The competition entry by Stoss Landscape Urbanism for Taichung Gateway Park, entitled "Aqua Cultures," presents a new park model that combines the establishment of recreational and cultural amenities with water treatment and the enhancement of biodiversity. Every year, Taiwan receives an average rainfall of 2,467 millimeters—more than the annual precipitation of the United States, India, and Australia combined. Despite this abundance, more than 50 percent of the rainfall is lost, primarily because of Taiwan's steep geography, tropical climate, and widespread urbanization in the lower elevation areas. These challenges also provide Taiwan with a rare opportunity to become an international leader in ecological water management practices.

Through the integration of an innovative and symbiotic water treatment system, this project for Taichung's newest cultural park is designed to provide a sustainable vision and an evocative experience of water management for the rest of the world. "Aqua Cultures" is a living filter for water and air that catalyzes a robust range of urban programs. Recreational and cultural activities are planned to occur within, atop, and beside the pools of water. Floating lanterns are envisioned to flicker in the night, people in kayaks and canoes are thought to populate the lake on warm summer afternoons, and children could watch for fish in the dense reeds. The design intends to provide moments of quiet reflection next to the gurgling waters.

Perspectival rendering of pools along the central spine of the park.

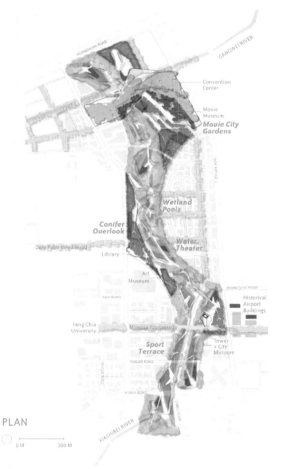

PLAN

Park design in context.

NZJ

Orange County Great Park, Orange County, California, United States. Competition 2005.
Hargreaves Associates

Oblique aerial view of design in context.

Park design in context.

Water was the driving force behind the initial development of both the form and the program for the park designed on the site of the former Marine Corps Air Station El Toro near Irvine, in the arid climate of Southern California. Four primary landscape types that variably depend on the availability of water characterize the park design: native oak grassland, irrigated fields, riparian corridors, and a productive landscape. The native oak grassland occupies the majority of the site, weaving the park together. Irrigated fields are scattered throughout. The productive landscape honors the agricultural heritage of the region and functions as a self-sustaining economic and ecological resource for the park and its surrounding communities. Riparian habitats with diverse flora and fauna occupy low areas and the drainage corridors. Large areas for cultural events and the commemoration of the site's history are distributed throughout the park in patches, while other strips of land are reserved for a variety of sporting activities.

Perspectival rendering of the riparian zone.

Perspectival rendering of the reused runway.

Perspectival rendering of the orange groves.

SRF

Wetland restoration at the former Hamilton Army Airfield, Novato, California. Commenced 1999.
US Army Corps of Engineers, San Francisco District
California State Coastal Conservancy

Oblique aerial of partially submerged airfield.

The Hamilton Wetland Restoration Project was authorized by Congress in 1999 as an ecosystem restoration project to be carried out by the Army Corps of Engineers. The project involves nearly 1,052 hectares of land, of which 301 hectares constitute the former Hamilton Army Airfield. The airfield was closed in the 1980s and transferred to the California State Coastal Conservancy under the Base Realignment and Closure Act program. The land was once tidal marsh on the shore of San Pablo Bay that was diked and drained for farming in the late 1800s. In the 1920s, the airfield replaced the farm and then became a major base during the Korean and Vietnam wars.

Due to natural oxidation of the peat soils, the ground surface has subsided six feet below the average sea level. To restore the tidal marsh, the site has been filled with nearly six million cubic yards of clean sediment from dredging projects in the Bay Area. Between 2008 and 2011, dredged sediment, which would have otherwise been dumped in the bay and ocean, was pumped ashore to cover up the long-abandoned runway. In the fall of 2013, the Army Corps of Engineers graded parts of the site to create ponds and channels, and in April 2014, the outboard levee along the bay was opened to the tides to complete the project, which entered a 13-year monitoring and management phase.

Pipelines of drainage system.

Cells for wetland restoration.

Airport Afterlives

Decommissioned airports have provided opportunities to reclaim, restore, and reconstruct large stretches of land as habitat. The projects featured in this section build on the natural and cultural heritage of the former airfield site. Layers of the site's history are unearthed and used as generators for design and restoration plans. The creation of new habitats for wildlife is paired with the design of environments for recreational and public use.

At Crissy Field in San Francisco, a wetland and dune landscape has been restored in the context of a cultural landmark. The Orange County Great Park design creates a wildlife corridor and various habitats as well as a veterans' memorial and other elements that recall the former air station's history. At Northerly Island in Chicago, the closure of the airport allows designers to propose new wildlife habitats while converting other areas into destinations for recreation and cultural events. The landscape plan for the Midway Island Atoll in the Pacific Ocean proposes to demolish runways and reestablish the native habitat for endangered marine species by turning the islands into a research center and a destination for ecotourism.

JFO

Crissy Field, San Francisco, United States. Completed 2001.
Hargreaves Associates

Aerial photograph.

Located on a filled salt marsh in the San Francisco Bay, Crissy Field was the first Air Coast Defense Station on the Pacific coast. Built between 1919 and 1925 on the vacant site of the 1915 Panama-Pacific International Exposition, the early airfield was a wide grassy expanse that soon became a landmark in early aviation history. In 1924, the first successful dawn-to-dusk transcontinental flight ended there, and in 1927 the first nonstop flight from the continental United States to Hawaii departed from the airfield. An asphalt-paved airstrip was built in 1936 to accommodate technologically advanced aircraft. Crissy Field closed to fixed-wing aircraft in 1974, and was decommissioned and turned over to the National Park Service (NPS) in 1994. By then, aircraft fuels and cleaning chemicals had heavily contaminated the site and the dumping of toxins had destroyed much of the marshland. The NPS worked with the Golden Gate National Parks

Association (today Golden Gate National Parks Conservancy) and a range of community stakeholders to remediate and prepare the site for its redevelopment into an urban park, which opened in 2001.

The conversion of the United States Sixth Army's military installation at the Presidio into a national park encompassed the restoration and rehabilitation of the natural landscape of wetlands and dune fields along the San Francisco Bay waterfront. Hargreaves Associates reintroduced the convoluted landforms, which in the past were generated by bracing wind and wave attacks on an otherwise relentlessly flat site, as sculpted landforms. Crissy Field enables a diversity of recreational uses in the dynamic environment of restored wetlands and within the context of an enduring historical landmark.

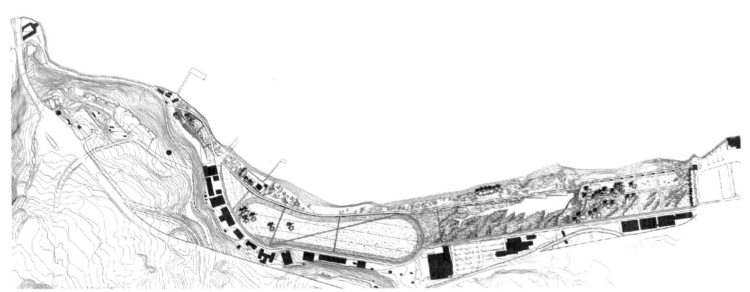

Park design in context.

Landform, aerial view.

Landform, aerial view.

Restored wetland.

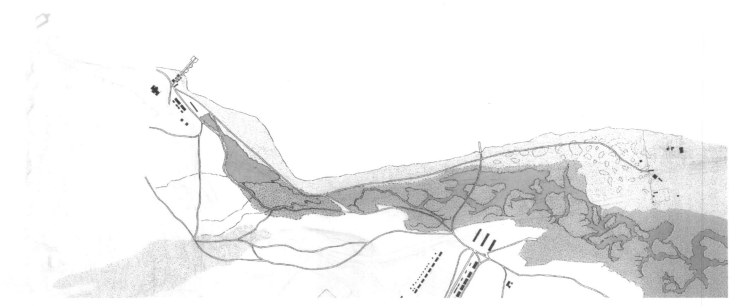

Wetlands, 1851–1857.

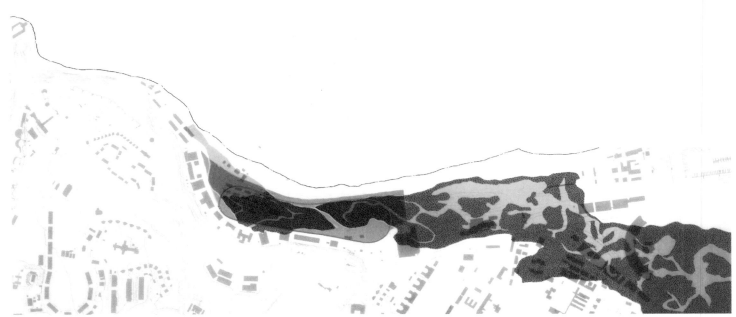

Overlay of wetlands and airfield.

CGX

Northerly Island Framework Plan, Chicago, United States. 2010.
Studio Gang Architects
JJR

Perspectival rendering showing an oblique aerial view of design in context.

Merrill C. Meigs Field Airport on Chicago's Northerly Island peninsula closed in 2003 and is to be turned into a new urban park, extending Chicago's system of lakefront parks. Studio Gang Architects' LEED Gold–targeted 2010 framework plan for Northerly Island reenvisions these 37 hectares on Chicago's lakefront, returning the land to public open space and constructing a topography and landscape that will enable wildlife to occupy the peninsula. The plan seeks to mix the "wild" with the constructed, providing a space for recreation, education, and wildlife habitation. The new park is designed to provide more active recreational uses in the north, as well as more passive uses that require secluded areas in the south. In the north, a new outdoor music amphitheater connects to the adjacent museum campus and can be used as a skating rink in the winter. In the southern half of the peninsula, the design suggests the construction of a wetland and savanna. Boardwalks and floating docks bring people close to the water. East of the peninsula, a reef is to be constructed, creating a lagoon and fish-spawning habitat. The completion of Phase I of the plan is anticipated for 2015.

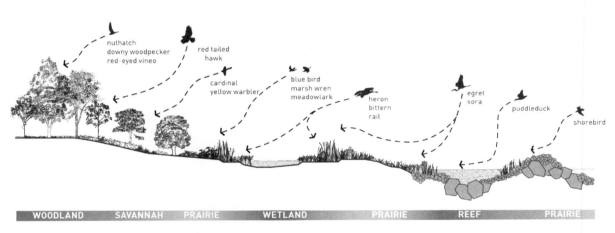

Section showing the diverse bird habitats.

Perspectival rendering illustrating the planned constructed lagoon and reef.

NZJ

Orange County Great Park, Orange County, Irvine, California, United States. Competition 2005.
Master Plan 2006. Preview Park 2007–2010. Palm Court & North Lawn 2011.
Ken Smith Landscape Architect
Mia Lehrer and Associates

Perspectival rendering showing an oblique aerial view of design in context.

Ken Smith Landscape Architect led the multidisciplinary team that won the 2005 design competition for the reuse of 545 hectares of the decommissioned Marine Corps Air Station El Toro as a metropolitan park serving the Southern California region. The Great Park design emphasizes sustainability at a large scale, seeking to create both wildlife habitats and a new social space that fosters community and health, regional identity, and a sense of history. The design proposes a canyon that winds through the site from the northwest to the southeast, and a 72-hectare wildlife corridor that connects the park with the Cleveland National Forest and is off-limits to park visitors. The remaining park areas are to provide for a variety of recreational pursuits, including hiking and biking, and for sustainable agriculture and related educational facilities. At the recently opened Palm Court Arts Complex, located on the site's earliest Marine Corps squadron unit, an iconic palm grove emphasizes the historic bowstring truss hangar and its two flanking warehouses that have been restored and adapted for contemporary use as an arts center.

Runway removal studies. The existing runways account for 79 hectares. Removing 85 percent of the runways reduces paving to 11.85 hectares. Removal of further 50 percent leaves 5.9 hectares that can be used for a military memorial and park circulation.

Bridge section.

MDY

Henderson Field Airport, Sand Island, Midway Atoll, United States territory. Conceptual site plan 2008. Jones & Jones Architects and Landscape Architects, Ltd.

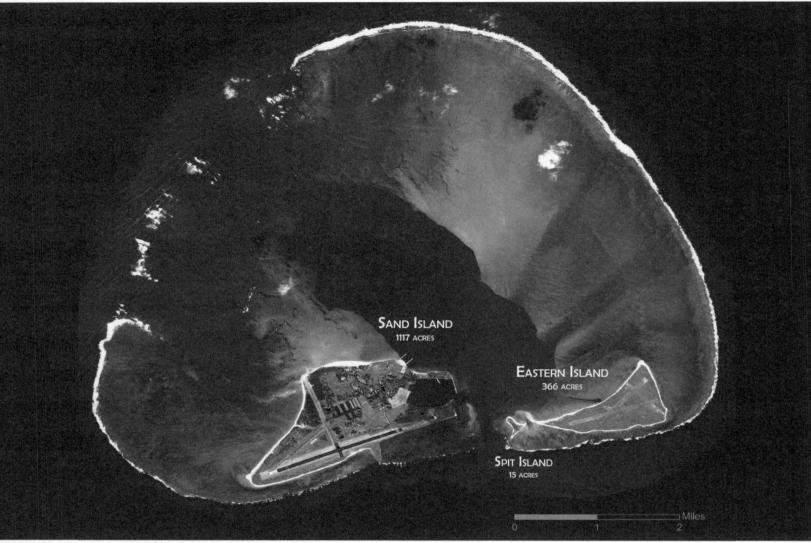

Satellite image showing the island atoll and the airstrips on Sand and Eastern Islands.

MDY

Built in 1940 to 1941 by the US Navy, the airstrip on Eastern Island and parts of the airstrip on Sand Island are to be demolished for the restoration of the Laysan albatross's native habitat and that of other endangered marine species found on Midway Atoll. Midway Atoll is part of the Papahānaumokuākea Marine National Monument, a 2,250-kilometer-long chain of uninhabited islands and atolls northwest of the main Hawaiian Islands that was established in 2006 by presidential proclamation. The Papahānaumokuākea Marine National Monument encompasses an area that is larger than all US national parks combined, and has the largest concentration of Laysan albatross in the world. Part of a volcanically created and subsiding island chain, Midway is an example of atoll formation, a poorly understood geological process. Shedding light on this process could contribute to better

understanding the relationship between climate, carbon sequestration, and reef development. Because of the occurrence of heat-induced coral bleaching and Midway's remote location in the middle North Pacific, it is an important node in the global network of biogeographical and oceanographic research. The plan envisions the islands as a site for limited ecotourism, education, and biological research by the US Fish and Wildlife Service, the National Oceanic and Atmospheric Administration, the state of Hawaii, and other partners. Nature-based tourism would focus on Midway's fragile ecosystems, marine resources, and historical significance, from the laying of the Pacific cable in 1903 to its strategic importance during World War II.

Laysan albatross chick on Sand Island, 2008.

Project Credits and Sources

Listed in order of appearance

AMS
Amsterdam Airport Schiphol, The Netherlands, 1992, construction 1994–1998. West 8 Urban Design & Landscape Architecture: Adriaan Geuze, Maarten Buijs, Cor Geluk, David Buurma, Dirry de Bruin, Edwin van der Hoeven, Erik Overdiep, Esther Kruit, Jelle Therry, Katrien Prak, Paul van Beek, Perry Maas.
West 8 Urban Design & Landscape Architecture; Amsterdam Airport Schiphol, "Schiphol: A Model of 'The Dutch Way.'" http://www.schiphol.nl /web/file?uuid=32a30e4a-c337-4dcb-b493- 329ebd9afe66&owner=7ccedf61-a8f4-4180-b5b0- 849e8def7d3e; Wouter Reh, Clemens Steenbergen, and Diederik Aten, *Sea of Land* (Wormer: Stichting Uitgeverij Noord-Holland, 2007).

MUC
Munich Airport, Germany, 1976–1992. Grünplan GmbH. Collaborators, consultants: *phytosociology* Dr. B. Dancau, Bayerische Landesanstalt für Bodenkunde und Pflanzenbau; *zoology* Dr. H. Ellenberg; *ornithology* Dr. W. Keil, Dr. E. Bezzel; *agriculture* Prof. Dr. R. Zapf; Flughafen München GmbH; Grünplan GmbH.

OSL
Oslo Airport, Gardermoen, Norway, 1989–1998. Aviaplan Architects, Engineers, and Landscape Architects, Bjørbekk & Lindheim AS (landscape master plan), 13.3 Landscape Architects (landscape details).
Competition for terminal expansion, 2008–2009. Team T2 Engineering Group, Nordic Office of Architecture, Bjørbekk & Lindheim AS. Bjørbekk & Lindheim AS; Gisle Erlien, "Gardermoen-mål for arkitekturen," *Byggekunst* 1 (1999): 16–19; Gudmund Stokke, "Oslo Lufthavn Gardermoen-Helhetsplan," *Byggekunst* 1 (1999): 13–15.

AKL
Auckland Airport, Auckland, New Zealand, commenced 2007. Surfacedesign, Inc.: James Lord, Garrett Miller, Geoff Di Girolamo, David Godshall. Collaborators, consultants: *local engineering* Harrison and Grierson, *local landscape* Bespoke: Lee Brazier, *Auckland City Council*: Lee Anderson and Lucia Tugaga.

CALUMET
Lake Calumet Airport and Southeast Chicago Environmental Plan, 1990–1992. City of Chicago, Office of Mayor Richard M. Daley. Collaborators, consultants: *aviation* Ricondo & Associates;

Landrum and Brown, *environmental planning* Hey & Associates, *economic development* Camiros, Ltd., *construction and cost planning* Skidmore, Owings & Merrill, *economic analysis* National Economic Research Associates; Geoff Goldberg, former Project Director, City of Chicago.

Runway Section
Massachusetts Port Authority

Windsock
US Department of Transportation, Federal Aviation Administration. AC No. 150/5345- 27D (6/2/04). Transport Canada. "TP 312–Aerodromes Standards and Recommended Practices (revised 03/2005)." http://www.tc.gc.ca/eng/civilaviation /publications/tp312- menu-4765.htm.

Eelgrass and Terns
San Diego County Regional Airport Authority, "The California Least Tern at San Diego International Airport." http://www.san.org/sdcraa/airport _initiatives/ environmental/protection/natural _resources.aspx.
Unified Port of San Diego, "Natural Resources and Wildlife. California Least Tern Updates and Photos." http://www.portofsandiego.org /environment/natural-resources/367-california-least-tern-updates-and-photos.html.

Goats
Monica Guzman, "Sea-Tac Airport Get Goats to Do the Weeding," *Seattle PI*, September 9, 2008. http://blog.seattlepi.com/thebigblog/2008/09/09 / sea-tac-airport-gets-goats-to-do-the-weeding/.
Jason Kayser, "Baa! O'Hare Turns to Goats to Clear Airfield Brush," *Associated Press*, August 13, 2013. http://bigstory.ap.org/article/baa-ohare-turns-goats-clear-airfield-brush.
Angela Kellner, "Bend Airport Hires a Goat Herd to Control Weeds." KLCC 89.7 FM, July 30, 2009. http://www.klcc.org/Feature.asp?FeatureID= 1240.
Scott Mayerowitz, "San Francisco International Airport Hires Goats to Prevent Fires," *HuffPost Los Angeles*, July 5, 2013. http://www.huffington-post.com/ 2013/07/06/san-francisco-international-airport-goats_n_3555096.html.
US Fish and Wildlife Service, "Managing Invasive Plants." http://www.fws.gov/invasives/stafftrain-ingmodule/methods/grazing/introduction.html.

Llamas
Ellen Jean Hirst, "O'Hare's Grass Gives Burros, Llamas, Goats, and Sheep Something to Chew On," *Chicago Tribune*, August 13, 2013.
Jason Kayser, "Baa! O'Hare Turns to Goats to Clear

Airfield Brush," *Associated Press*, August 13, 2013. http://bigstory.ap.org/article/baa-ohare-turns-goats-clear-airfield-brush.
Amy Schneider, "Sheep, Goats Munch on Airport Land," *Hartsfield-Jackson News*, October 2012. http://www.atlanta-airport.com/HJN/2012/10 /business2.htm.

Coyote Decoy
Rosemary Parker, "Coyote Fear Factor Used to Scare Animals from Kalamazoo Airport Runways," MLive, August 12, 2013. http://www.mlive.com /news/kalamazoo/ index.ssf/2013/08/hold_wylie _coyote_long_dead_us.html.

Peregrine Falcon
Barry Newman, "Falcons at New York's JFK Airport Join the Flock of the Unemployed," *Wall Street Journal*, April 29, 2011.
Stefan Ulrich, "Die Himmelfeger," *Süddeutsche Zeitung*, May 17, 2010.
Miriam Opresnik, "Falken für die Flugsicherung," *Hambuger Abendblatt*, December 28, 2004.
Transport Canada, "TP 13549–Sharing the Skies (March 2004)." http://www.tc.gc.ca/eng /civilaviation/publications/tp13549-menu-2163.htm. Records of the Federal Aviation Administration, Record Group 237, National Archives at College Park.

RoBird
Clear Flight Solutions, Nico Nijenhuis; Daniel Michaels, "It's a Bird, It's a Plane, It's a Robotic Bald Eagle," *Wall Street Journal*, June 16, 2010.

Sound Cannon
Transport Canada. "TP–Wildlife Control Procedures Manual." (January 2002). http://www.tc.gc.ca/eng /civilaviation/publications/tp11500-menu-1630.htm.
Federal Aviation Administration. "Wildlife Hazard Mitigation Program." http://www.faa.gov/airports /airport_safety/wildlife/management/.
Deutscher Ausschuss zur Verhütung von Vogelschlägen im Luftverkehr e.V. "DAVVL e.V. Arbeitsgruppe Flughafenökologie." http://www.davvl.de/de/verein/ arbeitsgruppen /flughafenoekologie.

Tall Fescue Grass
Carly Baldwin, "New York Senator Wants More Geese Killed after Second Plane Strike," *Metro. US*, April 25, 2012. http://www.metro.us/newyork /news/local/2012/04/25/new-york-senator-wants-more-geese-killed-after-second-plane-strike/#sthash.JuzPKoGv.dpuf.
Ingrid Hipkiss, "Kiwi Grass Reduces Bird-Strikes

Worldwide." *3News*, March 21, 2013. http://
www.3news.co.nz/Kiwi-grass-reduces-bird-
strikes-worldwide/tabid/1160/articleID/291276
/Default.aspx.
Television New Zealand, One News, "Bird-Deterring
Grass Could Solve Airport Woes." August6, 2011.
http://tvnz.co.nz/national-news/bird-deterring-
grass-could-solve-airport-woes-4341084.
Brian E. Washburn and Thomas W. Seamans,
"Foraging Preferences of Canada Geese Among
Turfgrasses: Implications for Reducing Human–
Goose Conflicts," *Journal of Wildlife Management*
76, no. 3 (2012): 600–607.

TXG
Taichung Gateway Park, Taichung, Taiwan.
Competition 2011: Mosbach Paysagistes, Philippe
Rahm architects, Ricky Liu Associates.
Consultants: Atelier LD, BETVRD, *climate
engineering* Transsolar, *structural engineering*
Bollinger + Grohmann, *light sculptor* Patrick
Rimoux, *hydraulic engineering* Sepia Conseils.
Mosbach Paysagistes; Taichung City Government,
Urban Development Bureau, "Taichung Shueinan
Airport Planning Project," November 15, 2011.
http://eng.taichung.gov.tw/ct.aspx?xItem=5321&
ctNode=1290 &mp=9.
"Air Force Airport Handed Over to Taichung," *China
Post*, December 23, 2007. http://www.chinapost.
com.tw/taiwan/local/taichung/ 2007/12/23/135996
/Air-force.htm.

GWW
Park Landscape and Urban Agriculture Gatow,
Gatow, Germany, competition 2010–2011. Büro
Kiefer Landschaftsarchitektur Berlin: Prof.
Gabriele G. Kiefer, Tancredi Capatti, Mathias
Staubach. Collaborators: Andreas Westendorf,
Robyn Butcher, Katrin Unger.

UIO
Parque Bicentenario, Quito, Ecuador, competition
2008. 2008 Parque del Lago Competition and
Park Conception: Ernesto X. Bilbao, Robert A.
Sproull, Jr.; 2012 Parque Bicentenario Master Plan:
Studio Ernesto Bilbao; 2030 Plan: Ernesto X.
Bilbao, Carolina Hidalgo; 2012-2013-2014-2020
Phases: Ernesto X. Bilbao. Collaborators, consul-
tants: Karen Román, Andrea Yépez, Fernando
Bucheli, Ana Sevilla, María de los Ángeles
Espinosa, Francisca Tapia, *botany* Carlos Ruales,
graphic design Esteban Calderón, *sanitary engi-
neering* Richard Aguirre, *electrical engineering*
Rubén Boada, *sustainability* Carolina Proaño.
Ernesto X. Bilbao, Robert A. Sproull, Jr.

RKV
Reykjavík Airport, Vatnsmýri, Iceland, competition
2007. Lateral Office.

EDNO
Oldenburg Airbase Solar Farm, Oldenburg, Germany,
2011. IFE Eriksen AG.

THF
Berlin Tempelhof Airport, Berlin, Germany, competi-
tion 2010. GROSS.MAX., Sutherland Hussey
Architects. Local coordination: WES & Partner
Landschaftsarchitekten, Ingenieurgesellschaft
Prof. Dr. Sieker mbH
GROSS.MAX.; Philipp Meuser, *Vom Fliegerfeld zum
Wiesenmeer* (Berlin: Quintessenz Verlag, 2000).

FBU
Oslo Airport, Fornebu, Oslo, Norway, 2004–2008.
Bjørbekk & Lindheim Landskapsarkitekter.
Consultants: *water artist* Atelier Dreiseitl,
technical Norconsult, Svein Erik Bergem, Simen
Gylseth, Knut H. Wiik, Elin Liavik, Line Løvstad
Nordbye, Håvard Strøm, Rune Vik, Christer
Ohlsson.

MUC
Landscape Park Munich-Riem, Germany, 1995–2006.
Latitude Nord. Gilles Vexlard and Laurence
Vacherot. Local Coordination: Stahr &
Haberland; Luz Landschaftsarchitekten
München.

LA CARLOTA
Generalísimo Francisco de Miranda Air Base, La
Carlota, Caracas, Venezuela, competition 2012.
Anita Berrizbeitia, Luis Callejas, Somatic
Collaborative/Felipe Correa, Lucas Correa, Elias
Gonzalez, Mariusz Klemens, Pablo Perez Ramos,
Andrew McGee.

CAS
Anfa Airport, Casablanca, Morocco, commenced
2007. Agence Ter, Reichen et Robert & Associés.

RKV
Vatnsmýri, Reykjavík, Iceland, competition 2007.
Graeme Massie Architects.

DEN
Stapleton Redevelopment, Denver, Colorado,
commenced 1997. Lead landscape architecture
firm: AECOM.
AECOM; Russell Fortmeyer, "An Abandoned Airport
Brownfield Takes Off," *Architectural Record* 194,

no. 7 (2006): 147–150,152,154; City and County of
Denver, Stapleton Redevelopment Foundation,
Citizens Advisory Board, *Stapleton Development
Plan: Integrating Jobs, Environment and Community*
(Denver, CO: City and County of Denver, 1995).

NOP
Floyd Bennett Field. National Park Service, Ashley
Scott Kelly and Rikako Wakabayashi
Sarah K. Cody and J. Auwaerter, *Cultural Landscape
Report for Floyd Bennett Field*, State University of
New York (Boston: National Park Service, 2009).
Kate Orff, Sarah Williams, Tse-Hui Teh, and Li-Chi-
Wang, *Envisioning Gateway Research Report*,
Columbia University Graduate School of
Architecture, Planning, and Preservation (New
York, 2007).
Regional Plan Association and National Parks
Conservation Association, "The Path Forward:
Public Input on the Future of the Gateway
National Recreation Area" (Fall 2009). http://
www.rpa.org/pdf/ GNRA_RPA_Report.pdf.

YZD
Downsview Park, Toronto, Canada, competition
1999. Bernard Tschumi Architects: Bernard
Tschumi, Robert Holton, Maia Small, Valentin
Bontjes van Beek. Toronto: Dereck Revington
Studio and Sterling Finlayson Architects.
Landscape: Gunta Mackars
Bernard Tschumi Architects; Julia Czerniak, ed.,
Downsview Park Toronto (Cambridge, MA,
Munich: Harvard University Graduate School of
Design, Prestel Verlag, 2001).

JOHANNISTHAL
Landscape Park Johannisthal, Berlin, Germany, 1996,
construction 1998–2010. Büro Kiefer
Landschaftsarchitektur Berlin.

THF
Berlin Tempelhof Airport, Berlin, Germany,
competition 2010. Topotek 1, Dürig AG.

YZD
Downsview Park, Toronto, Canada, competition
1999. James Corner/Field Operations; Stan Allen,
Stan Allen Architect; Michael Horsham, Tomato.
Consultants: *engineering* Craig Schwitter, Buro
Happold *landscape architecture* David Dutot, The
Delta Group, *lighting design* Herve Descottes,
L'Observatoire International, *storm-water and
environmental management* Tom Cahill and
Michelle Adams, Tom Cahill Associates, *economic
strategy* Chris Zlocki, HLWStrategies, *horticul-
ture* Chris Graham, Royal Botanical Gardens, *art
consultant* Marc Mayer, The Powerplant

Contemporary Art Gallery, *geography/local information* Edward Relph, University of Toronto, *ecology* Tom Siccama, Yale School of Forestry; Nina-Marie Lister, University of Toronto, *research and support* Penn Praxis, University of Pennsylvania.

SQUANTUM
Squantum Point Park, Quincy, Massachusetts, United States, 1997–2001. Carol R. Johnson Associates.
Carol R. Johnson Associates; Department of Conservation and Recreation of the Commonwealth of Massachusetts.

ATH
Hellenikon Metropolitan Park and Urban Development, Athens, competition, 2005.
Philippe Coignet/Office of Landscape Morphology, Paris; Elena Fernandez + David Serero Architects. Collaborators, consultants: Erwin Redl, Ryosuke Shimoda, Dominik Sigg, Takuma Kakehi, Yves Ubelmann, Silvia Zagheno, Davide Costelli, Valia Petraki, Stella Daouti.
Office of Landscape Morphology, Paris; Canadian Center for Architecture, "Eero Saarinen Athens Airport Collection." http://www.cca.qc.ca/en /collection/1078-eero-saarinen-athens-airport.

UIO
Mariscal Sucre International Airport, Quito, Ecuador, 2008.
Anita Berrizbeitia, Danilo Martic, Sebastián Hernández, and Andrea Masuero.

UIO
Mariscal Sucre International Airport, Quito, Ecuador, 2008. Luis Callejas (LCLA), Edgar Mazo, and Sebastian Mejia (Paisajes Emergentes).

TXG
Taichung Gateway Park, Taichung, Taiwan, competition 2011. Stoss Landscape Urbanism. Collaborators, consultants: *local coordination and architecture* Shu Chang Associates Architects, *sustainability, engineering* Arup, *graphics* Project Projects, *planting* Hang-Ming Hsia.

NZJ
Orange County Great Park, Orange County, California, United States, competition 2005. Hargreaves Associates.

SRF
Wetland restoration at the former Hamilton Army Airfield, commenced 1999.
US Army Corps of Engineers, San Francisco District; California State Coastal Conservancy.

JFO
Crissy Field, San Francisco, United States, completed 2001. Hargreaves Associates.
Hargreaves Associates; National Park Service, "Crissy Field." http://www.nps.gov/prsf/historyculture /crissy-field.htm.
Kirt Rieder, "Crissy Field: Tidal Marsh Restoration and Form," *Manufactured Sites*, ed. Niall Kirkwood (London and New York: Taylor and Francis, 2001), 193–205.

CGX
Northerly Island Framework Plan, Chicago, United States, 2010. Studio Gang Architects. Collaborators, consultants: *landscape architecture/ coastal engineering* JJR, ecology Applied Ecological Services, Inc.; *financial consulting* Applied Real Estate Analysis, Inc. Sustainability engineering: dbHMS; *consulting* Fish Transportation Group, Inc.; *graphic design* Studio V Design, Inc.

NZJ
Orange County Great Park, Orange County, Irvine, California, United States, competition 2005, master plan 2006, preview park 2007–2010, Palm Court & North Lawn 2011. Master plan and comprehensive design team: *master designer/landscape architect/team lead* Ken Smith Landscape Architect, *landscape architecture* Mia Lehrer and Associates, *project management* Gafcon, *architecture* TENArquitectos, *civil engineering* Fuscoe Engineering, *structural/sustainable engineer* Buro Happold, *ecological systems* Green Shield Ecology, Inc., *art integration* Mary Miss Studio, *traffic and circulation analysis* LSAAssociates, *water systems* Aquatic Design Group, *lighting design* Jim Conti Lighting Design, *water features* Fluidity Design Consultants, *signage and wayfinding* Made In Space, *irrigation systems* DDPagano, *soils analysis* Wallace Labs. WORKSHOP: Ken Smith Landscape Architect.

MDY
Henderson Field Airport, Sand Island, Midway Atoll, United States territory, conceptual site plan 2008. Jones & Jones Architects and Landscape Architects, Ltd.

Image Credits

7–8 Courtesy of Regency Enterprises and Photofest
12 Bernard Tschumi Architects, Dereck Revington Studio, Sterling Finlayson
17 James Corner Field Operations
22 West 8 Urban Design & Landscape Architecture
23 West 8 Urban Design & Landscape Architecture
24 West 8 Urban Design & Landscape Architecture
25 West 8 Urban Design & Landscape Architecture
26 Flughafen München GmbH
27 Flughafen München GmbH
28 Ole A. Krogness
29 Ivan Brody
30 Surfacedesign, Inc.
31 Surfacedesign, Inc.
32 G. Goldberg + Associates
33 G. Goldberg + Associates
36 Massachusetts Port Authority, Capital Programs and Environmental Affairs Department
37 (left) Federal Aviation Administration; (right) Massachusetts Office of Coastal Zone Management
38 AP Photo/Jason Keyser
39 (left) AP Photo/Jason Keyser; (right) Harvard University Graduate School of Design/photo Justin Knight
40 Harvard University Graduate School of Design/ photo Justin Knight
41 GreenX via UAS Vision
42 Margo Supplies, Ltd.
43 Harry Rose via Flickr
46–49 2015 Andreas Gursky / Artists Rights Society (ARS), New York / VG Bild-Kunst, Bonn
50–53 Vera Lutter
54–57 Hubert Blanz
58–61 Richard Mosse
62–67 Jeffrey Milstein
68–71 Alex MacLean
72–77 Yann Arthus-Bertrand
78–83 Robert Burley
84–89 Kathleen Shafer
90–95 Phil Underdown
96 State of Hawaii Department of Transportation, Airports Division
98 *Consulting Engineer* 41, September 1973, title page
99 US National Archives and Records Administration, RG 237-G, Records of the Federal Aviation Administration, General Photographic File, 1986–1995, Box 6, Folder 43
101 Frances Loeb Library, Harvard University Graduate School of Design
102 Frances Loeb Library, Harvard University Graduate School of Design
104 State of Hawaii Department of Transportation, Airports Division
107 US National Archives and Records Administration, RG 237, Federal Aviation Administration, CAA, Miscellaneous Records of Colonel Sumpter Smith, 1935–46, Box 3
110 Smithsonian Institution Archives. SIA2014-

07445, Acc 04–086, Box 2, Folder 5
114 National Park Service, Everglades National Park [image nos. EVER 12735 and EVER 12998]
117 (top) Institut für Stadtgeschichte Frankfurt am Main. S7Z1980, 256; (bottom) US National Archives and Records Administration, RG 237, Federal Aviation Administration, CAA, Miscellaneous Records of Colonel Sumpter Smith, 1935–46, Box no. 3
122 Cyrille Thomas
123 Cyrille Thomas
124 Mosbach Paysagistes
125 (left) Mosbach Paysagistes; (right) Cyrille Thomas
126 Senatsverwaltung für Stadtentwicklung Berlin
127 Büro Kiefer Landschaftsarchitektur Berlin
128 Ernesto Xavier Bilbao and Robert Andrew Sproull, Jr.
129 Ernesto Xavier Bilbao and Robert Andrew Sproull, Jr.
130 Lateral Office
131 Lateral Office
132 Alex MacLean
133 IFE Eriksen AG
134 IFE Eriksen AG/photo: Stephan Meyer-Bergfeld
135 IFE Eriksen AG/photo: Stephan Meyer-Bergfeld
138 GROSS.MAX.
139 GROSS.MAX.
140 GROSS.MAX.
141 GROSS.MAX.
142 Bjørbekk & Lindheim Landskapsarkitekter
143 Bjørbekk & Lindheim Landskapsarkitekter
144 MRG
145 (left) Latitude Nord; (right) MRG
146 Anita Berrizbeitia et al.
147 Anita Berrizbeitia et al.
148 Agence Ter
149 Agence Ter
150 Reykjavíkurborg—Skipulags- og byggingarsvið
151 Graeme Massie Architects
152 AECOM
153 Forest City/photo Ken Redding
154 Joe Mabel
155 Ashley Scott Kelly and Rikako Wakabayashi
158 Bernard Tschumi Architects, Dereck Revington Studio, Sterling Finlayson
159 Bernard Tschumi Architects, Dereck Revington Studio, Sterling Finlayson
160 Bernard Tschumi Architects, Dereck Revington Studio, Sterling Finlayson
161 Bernard Tschumi Architects, Dereck Revington Studio, Sterling Finlayson
162 Adlershof Projekt GmbH/photo: Dirk Laubner
163 Büro Kiefer Landschaftsarchitektur Berlin
164 Büro Kiefer Landschaftsarchitektur Berlin
165 Sonja Dümpelmann
166 Topotek 1
167 Topotek 1

168 Canada Lands Company
169 James Corner Field Operations
170 Alex MacLean
171 Carol R. Johnson Associates/photo Jerry Howard
174 Office of Landscape Morphology, Paris
175 Office of Landscape Morphology, Paris
176 Office of Landscape Morphology, Paris
177 Office of Landscape Morphology, Paris
178 Anita Berrizbeitia et al.
179 Anita Berrizbeitia et al.
180 Paisajes Emergentes
181 Paisajes Emergentes
182 Paisajes Emergentes
183 Paisajes Emergentes
184 Stoss Landscape Urbanism
185 Stoss Landscape Urbanism
186 Hargreaves Associates
187 Hargreaves Associates
188 US Army Corps of Engineers, San Francisco District
189 (left) US Army Corps of Engineers, San Francisco District; (right) Tom Gandesbery, CA State Coastal Conservancy
192 Hargreaves Associates
193 Hargreaves Associates
194 Hargreaves Associates
195 Hargreaves Associates
196 Studio Gang Architects
197 Studio Gang Architects
198 WORKSHOP: Ken Smith Landscape Architect
199 WORKSHOP: Ken Smith Landscape Architect
200 Jones & Jones Architects and Landscape Architects, Ltd.
201 Forest and Kim Starr

About the Editors

SONJA DÜMPELMANN
is Associate Professor of Landscape Architecture at the Harvard University Graduate School of Design. She holds a PhD in Landscape Architecture from the University of the Arts, Berlin, and has held research fellowships at the German Historical Institute and at Dumbarton Oaks in Washington, DC. Her publications include *Flights of Imagination: Aviation, Landscape, Design* (University of Virginia Press, 2014); a book on the Italian landscape architect Maria Teresa Parpagliolo Shephard (VDG Weimar, 2004); the edited *Cultural History of Gardens in the Age of Empire* (Bloomsbury Publishers, 2013); and the co-edited *Women, Modernity, and Landscape Architecture* (Routledge, 2015) and *Greening the City: Urban Landscapes in the Twentieth Century* (University of Virginia Press, 2011).

CHARLES WALDHEIM
is the John E. Irving Professor of Landscape Architecture at the Harvard University Graduate School of Design, where he directs the school's Office for Urbanization. His research examines the relations between landscape, ecology, and contemporary urbanism. On these topics Waldheim is author of *Landscape as Urbanism: A General Theory* (Princeton University Press, 2016) and editor of *The Landscape Urbanism Reader* (Princeton Architectural Press, 2006). Waldheim is a recipient of the Rome Prize Fellowship from the American Academy in Rome; the Visiting Scholar Research Fellowship at the Study Centre of the Canadian Centre for Architecture; and the Sanders Fellowship at the University of Michigan.

Airport Landscape: Urban Ecologies in the Aerial Age
Sonja Dümpelmann, Charles Waldheim (eds.)

Design
    Sam de Groot
Editorial Support
    Melissa Vaughn, Carolyn Deuschle, Sara Gothard,
    Jake Starmer
Permissions
    Sara Gothard
Typeface Customization
    Dinamo.us
Printing
    Die Keure, Belgium
Distribution
    Harvard University Press
Cover Illustration
    Phil Underdown, *Grassland #45353*, 2009

Harvard Design Studies is a book series published by
the Harvard University Graduate School of Design

Dean and Alexander and Victoria Wiley Professor of Design
    Mohsen Mostafavi
Assistant Dean for Communications
    Benjamin Prosky
Editor in Chief
    Jennifer Sigler
Publications Coordinator
    Meghan Sandberg

Sponsored by John E. (Jack) Irving Dean's Innovation
Fund, Scruggs Fund

Special Thanks
    Michael Mann and Chad Oppenheim

ISBN 978-1-934510-47-6

Harvard University
Graduate School of Design
48 Quincy Street
Cambridge, MA 02138
gsd.harvard.edu

Library of Congress Cataloging-in-Publication Data
Sonja Duempelmann, editor. Charles Waldheim, editor.
Airport Landscape: Urban Ecologies in the Aerial Age /
    Sonja Duempelmann, Charles Waldheim, eds.
Cambridge: Harvard University Graduate School of
    Design, 2016. Series: Harvard Design Studies
Includes bibliographical references.
    LCCN 2016000314
    ISBN 9781934510476
    1. Airports—Design and construction—Case studies—
        Exhibitions. 2. Airports—Environmental aspects—
        Case studies—Exhibitions. 3. Urban Ecology
        (Sociology)—Case studies—Exhibitions. 4. Urban
        ecology (Biology)—Case studies—Exhibitions.
        5. Reclamation of land—Case studies—
        Exhibitions.
    LCC TL725.3.L6 A39 2016
    DDC 711/.78—dc23